Praise for Stronger than the Storms

Toni is a gift to the body of Christ, just as we all
are. But I'm discovering more of Toni's gift with
each new work she comes out with. In *Stronger than the
Storms,* Toni is honest, transparent and right in line
with the Word of the Lord. You will find scripture to
help you travel through whatever the storm is that
you are facing.

— Sharon Jolliff
Thriving Beyond the Borders
DISC Personality Consultant

I found *Stronger than The Storms* to be packed full of
God's truth. I love how Toni easily explains the
authority and power that lies within every one of
God's children if we would just dare to believe it,
obey it and act upon it. This is a must read for
anyone!

— Angela Logan
Pastor
Adoration Fellowship Church

Stronger than the Storms

DISCOVERING THE 3-STEP STRATEGY TO LIFELONG STRENGTH AND COURAGE

TONI CHISM

WARRIOR HOUSE

—

ISBN: 979-8-9852861-2-0 (paperback), 979-8-9852861-3-7 (e-book)

Stronger than the Storms: Discovering the 3-Step Strategy to Lifelong Strength and Courage

Subject: Spiritual Warfare

Published by Warrior House Publishing

Newcastle, OK 73065

www.tonichism.com

Cover Design, Text Design and Formatting: Writing Momentum LLC

Contents

My Gift to You

Hello beautiful builders! You've purchased *Stronger than the Storms* – now enjoy this **FREE PDF** workbook, normally $20, as my gift to you. It's filled with interactive questions, reflections and more ... all designed to help you build a life with God that's stronger than the storms.

To download your free **PDF** workbook, simply go here before this special offer ends:

ToniChism.com/workbook

To the One Who helps us be stronger than the storms.

Foreword

When I was growing up in Southwest Oklahoma, tornados were a constant threat. In fact, at just ten years old our house was destroyed by one.

Because of that, a fear of tornados and destruction grew inside me to the point where I was terrified every time it started to rain. I knew this wasn't something God did, but it didn't stop me from being afraid. I knew I had to step out, ON PURPOSE and face my fears or become a slave to that fear.

It took getting to know Jesus personally and understanding what He has done and the power and authority He has given to me to be delivered from that fear.

My dear friend, Toni Chism, explains this process beautifully in this book. I knew I was stronger than the storm because of Jesus and the authority He has given us.

As the Senior Pastor at The Sanctuary OK in Oklahoma City, I see the stronghold of fear daily in the lives of congregants, family, and friends.

Understanding what Jesus did on the cross, studying the word of God and realizing the power and authority He has bestowed on us, is what helps people break-free from the strongholds of fear. Being active and not inactive.

I am so thankful Toni wrote this book to help others understand that through God, you are stronger than the storm.

I can't promise that it will be easy. But I promise you that *Stronger than the Storms* is straight from God's Word and will help you understand what you already have through Christ.

Stevan Cunningham
Founder & Senior Pastor at Sanctuary OK
and Crowned One Ministries

CHAPTER 1
Storms Come

The behemoth tornado that barreled toward us was black. It roared like a freight train, leaving a trail of debris in its wake. It ripped roofs to shreds, demolished buildings, wrecked cars, and vacuumed horses and cows into its path of destruction. Unlike the one that carried Dorothy and her little dog into a far-away land called Oz, this enormous display of power flattened everything in its path. It wasn't the thin, rope-style tornado. Nor was it the traditional funnel shape. This monster appeared to be a spawn of hell.

Weather forecasters had warned that conditions were prime for massive twisters. I'd lived in Oklahoma long enough to know that tornadoes could drop from the sky on a whim during these times. Their route followed no known pattern. A tornado could twist north or rotate south. It could head for miles in one direction before taking a hard right turn to terrorize another route. Or even be sucked back into the sky.

This one did nothing of the sort. It continued straight toward us. I gripped the arm rest in our pickup and asked God how to outrun it. The truck shimmied as blackness loomed ever closer. The meteorologist shouted the term that no one wanted to hear.

EF5.

My husband floored the truck and headed south. The tornado traveled east, northeast, with winds more than 210 mph. I forced myself to look away and check on my three quiet granddaughters. Their brown eyes were as wide as mason jar lids. They'd always counted on me. I'd protected them, kissed their tears away, and kept them safe.

Without uttering a peep, their eyes darted between me and the tornado. My heart ached as they stared in terror. Their little faces sent chills up my spine as the storm kept whirling in front of us, filling the sky with its wrath.

It was my daughter Fallon's thirty-first birthday. That morning I'd been preparing the chicken for her favorite tacos for dinner. Her home where she was babysitting was in the storm's path, also. She heard the weatherman shout over the television. "Take shelter immediately. Get underground or get out of the way. *Tornado emergency! Tornado emergency! Tornado emergency!*"

The intensity of the tornado was such that no one in its path would survive above ground. There was no storm cellar in their home, so Fallon grabbed the three-year-old and jumped into their vehicle. With her husband behind the wheel, and the tornado in his rear-view mirror, they headed north toward Edmond in the pouring rain. Her anxiety lessened as the precious, little entertainer tugged on her ears, stuck out her tongue and laughed.

They were safe. That's all that mattered.

It took hours for them to make it back home. When they entered their neighborhood in south Oklahoma City, it was full of debris and downed trees. In their yard, though, there were only scattered leaves and a four-foot branch.

Although everything was ready for chicken tacos, none of us had an appetite. No one felt like celebrating. We sat in horror watching the aftermath on television. All I could do was mourn and pray for my neighboring town and for the people who fell victim to the storm. And be grateful.

I thanked God for His promises of protection. I thanked Him for teaching me how to keep His Word between my family and whatever storm threatened. It'd been my decades long habit to lay my hand on top of my children and grand-children's heads as I pled the Blood of Jesus, proclaimed God's promises of protection over them and prayed in the Spirit whenever He prompted.

That day, May 20, 2013, had begun like any other day. Mothers kissed their loved one's goodbye, never imagining that it was for the last time. The mile and a half wide tornado stayed on the ground for 14 miles. It destroyed much of the city of Moore, Oklahoma, and everything in its path. It wiped out two elementary schools. It destroyed 300 homes, numerous businesses and the hopes and futures of many. When it was over, 24 people had died and 212 were injured.

I was thankful we survived the storm but couldn't ignore the fact we'd come so close to what stole the lives of many. Not because I prayed better than others. Not because of luck or that God had favorites. Instead, I'd listened and obeyed when the Lord taught me how to put His Word between me, my loved ones and any potential threats. It was the Word of God's power working in our lives that made the difference in our outcome that day, and many other times.

Through Jesus Christ, we can be stronger than inevitable problems. Although this chaotic world teems with every kind of danger, Jesus calmed the raging storms and walked on rough waters.

Oh, that was Jesus, you say. Yes. However, God promised that if we believed, we'd do the same works that Jesus did.

"Most assuredly, I say to you, he who believes in Me, the *works* that I do he will do also; and greater works than these he will do, because I go to My Father" (John 14:12).

OBEDIENCE TO THE WORD OF THE LORD

Consider the land of Goshen in the book of Exodus. Egypt suffered ten plagues when Pharaoh refused to release the children of Israel. God's people who lived in Goshen were unharmed, protected even when the death angel killed all the first-born of Egypt. (Exodus 12:23 TLB).

For the Israelites, their obedience to do what God said— applying blood of a spotless lamb on their doorposts was symbolic of the Blood of Jesus. Literally, they put the Word of God (John 1:1,14) between them and the destroyer.

That's what my friend, Vicki Simmons had learned to do.

VICKI'S ENCOUNTER

Vicki struggled to steady her hand, May 20, 2013. Keeping her phone's camera still and in focus was a challenge as she videoed the EF5 tornado's aftermath.

Alone with her thoughts, she took a long, hard look at something she wasn't used to seeing. Devastation. Ruin. Utter sadness.

Birds hovered overhead. Chirping, and fluttering they found nowhere to roost. Amid heaps of debris and rubble that looked like a bomb had exploded, there was nowhere for them to take refuge.

Vicki knew the birds followed the Lord's wisdom. Birds were equipped with their own God-given storm tracking system and had a keen sense for shifting winds and temperature changes. In fact, they sought shelter as a storm approached. In this case, the birds may have navigated completely out of the monstrous storm and then returned when it had passed.

God took care of the birds by equipping them for what they needed to stay safe. They responded, sheltered, and survived the storm. That day, their chirping syllables and whistles seemed to search for contact, like a heart seeking the comfort of a familiar voice. Their survival was proof that He'd provided for their safekeeping. He'd done the same for Vicki. After all, she'd followed her own God-given guidance system long before the storm was on the horizon.

In syllables almost too painful to utter, she'd prayed for weeks ahead of this time.

"I'd wake up in the morning and be overwhelmed by the Holy Spirit. I had no idea what it was about. The only thing I could do was pray in the Spirit and weep."

Vicki referred to her prayer language, received through the Baptism of Holy Spirit. A language of syllables, utterances, and sounds. It's a divine GPS that takes us into the supernatural heart of God.

"God invites us into the realm that knows all things. Even though our understanding is limited, obeying what we hear in that realm keeps us from falling headlong into a danger zone," Vicki said.

Every morning for about two months, Vicki was obedient to utter syllables that God impressed upon her. She wept tears that poured like rain. Bawling and praying, she drove for several miles each day to the school where she was taking classes. "When I got there, I'd have to forcibly pull myself out of this so I could clean my face to go into the school and my classroom."

Her phone rang on the afternoon of May 20th while she was running an errand.

"Where are you?" Her friend's voice was urgent. "You need to get home! There's a big storm coming!"

Vicki wasn't alarmed. After all, she lived in Oklahoma. High winds and thunderstorms often rocked the state's atmosphere creating unstable conditions that brought the threat of tornados. At her friend's insistence that a big storm was fast approaching, though, Vicki headed home noticing that the western sky had become dark and ominous. After putting her car in park, she hurried inside her home and turned the television on just in time to hear, "Tornado on the ground in Moore!"

From the weathercaster's description of the storm's route, Vicki knew it was headed straight toward her. She had to get underground. Pausing for a quick glance around the room, she realized there wasn't time to gather anything. She ran out of the door, jumped into her car, and sped around the corner to her mother's house.

"We have to leave!" She shouted as she came in the door, then added, "You can't bring the dog!" Vicki couldn't believe what she was saying. She loved Peanut too. He'd circle her legs jumping with joy each time she visited. Vicki was part of Peanut's immediate family, though. The dog acted like a vicious animal around strangers. A knock on the door would bring Peanut into full assault mode, snarling and biting.

"We have to go now!" Vicki yelled, standing over her mother and brother who remained seated in the den.

Instead, they refused to leave, even as they watched the massive funnel cloud inch closer.

Vicki was stunned. "This monster storm barreled in our direction and still, they wouldn't leave without the dog!"

Vicki hated to leave the playful, white terrier behind. She knew, however, that the dog would bite the people in the shelter. Peanut couldn't handle being around outsiders. Her mother never took him out of the yard due to his aggression towards strangers. Add the storm and high anxiety levels, and it was a recipe for disaster.

Storm chasers screamed through the television. Panic gripped Vicki. Time was of the essence. Looking at the tornado, Vicki decided. "I begged them to come with me, but they wouldn't. There was no way I was willing to take a chance against that monster of a tornado. I walked out of my mom's house alone, feeling sick inside."

Brokenhearted, she ran through large hail to her car and drove away. "Looking back over my shoulder I could see the tornado covering the whole neighborhood. I thought, I've lost my mother. I've lost my family! Even though I'd done everything I could to convince them to leave, they'd refused. My heart totally sank."

Vicki was greeted by a locked door at the shelter. Distraught, she beat on the door hoping someone would hear her above the rock-like hail beating the ground. Finally, someone let her in.

"My heart was beating out of my chest. I tried to maintain control around the others, but I was worried about my mom and brother." She was grateful to be underground, but her family were protected only by their home.

After about thirty minutes in the hot, muggy shelter, the radio announcer said that the area had been cleared for people to leave their safe spots. Vicki had no idea what she'd find as she drove toward her mother's house. As she approached her neighborhood, the houses were still standing. "That's when I knew my mother was okay."

As impossible as it seemed, God had protected her mom, her brother and little Peanut.

"When I reached my house, I saw my neighbor's grandson, a sweet young man with Down syndrome. He stood on the driveway with lifted hands, praising God."

"Our houses are still here, but have you seen behind us?" the boy's grandfather asked.

"No, what happened?" Vicki said.

"It's gone. It isn't there anymore."

The EF5 tornado had spun behind her home. It hadn't crossed her doorstep.

The streets to her neighborhood and to her mother's house were clear and she had no trouble driving. The other side of Vicki's house was a different story. The street was full of debris, making it impossible to drive. She took off on foot, instead. Only two blocks away, nothing was standing.

"Everything was leveled. It was like a bomb had gone off. First responders couldn't even get in because of all the fallen utility lines."

Vicki could have been standing in a third world war zone for all she knew. Nothing looked familiar. "There were no road signs. I couldn't get my bearings. It was catastrophic."

People streamed in from the wreckage. Emerging out of nowhere, they seemed to come from every direction. Vicki and the others searched for survivors among the piles of rubble. It was haunting. Then she went home and prayed. She prayed for the Moore community and thanked God for His protection.

THE DIFFERENCE PRAYER MAKES

Vicki believes she wasn't the only one that God prompted to pray during those months leading up to the tornado. "The Lord moved on His children to intercede and that's what made the difference." She understands the human toll would have been much worse had she and the others not listened to the Lord and prayed. "What if the Lord moved on forty other people to intercede while He moved on me to pray? And I believe He did. What if only a few responded?"

My friend, Melanie Hemry, believes that God moved on many to intercede for the people of Moore, including her. For months she was burdened by a need to pray and intercede. She never knew what she was praying for until after the behemoth had passed.

"I cried and prayed in the spirit for two or three months before that monster struck. The only words I prayed that I understood were, Mama. Mama. Mama. Then I'd cry even more. Over and over, I said, Mama. Mama. Mama, as I prayed in tongues. It wasn't until after the tornado that I realized I'd been interceding for the children who were trapped and scared, crying for their mothers."

Melanie's face fell and her eyes became weepy as she told me of the moment when she realized that she'd been interceding for the children.

Thank you, Melanie and Vicki. Thank you to all the intercessors who yield to Holy Spirit's promptings and pray.

HEAR AND OBEY VERSES INACTION

According to disaster teams and law enforcement authorities, one of the biggest problems with destructive storms is public inaction. People don't take the threat seriously enough to act.

As God's kids we can choose to act whenever He prompts us. We can't afford inaction. The Moore tornado proved that many lives were saved because of the obedience of Melanie, Vicki and the others who heard the Lord's request for prayer.

"The Spirit realm touches the natural realm," Vicki said. "We're invited to participate in both realms. Sometimes we miss it. We're too busy or pre-occupied and we don't yield to what God asks us to do. God's call to intercede is often attached to the preservation of life. In this case, His intercessors cooperated, and lives were saved."

Obedience to God's voice is critical. We must hear what He says and "Just do it."

Sounds like Jesus. He said a wise man is one who hears His voice and obeys (Matthew 7:24-25).

After the tornado, neither Vicki or Melanie had the overwhelming urge to pray and intercede like they had over those few months. Melanie didn't live in the area affected by the tornado. Vicki's car and the roof of her home were totaled, although when the hail beat all around, it never touched her. She didn't have any bruises or welts. It was as if she wore an invisible forcefield that protected her.

That afternoon on May 20th, Melanie, Vicki, me, our families, and countless others witnessed what God is so famous for—His goodness.

That's what Moses saw on the outside of his prayer tent one evening while leading the Israelites into the Promised Land. "Please," Moses asked. "Show me Your glory."

Then God said, "I will make all My goodness pass before you…" (Exodus 33:18-19).

God could be anything that He wanted to be. He chose to be good.

God's goodness even extends to the birds (Matthew 6:26). His protection, love and goodness are always running after us. We can train ourselves to listen for His voice, and then obey.

"Sacrifice and offering You do not desire, *nor* have You delight in them: You have given me the capacity to hear *and* obey…" (Psalm 40:6 AMPC).

MULTITUDES OF STORMS

While we live in dangerous times, storms are not new. Jesus said there would be wars and rumors of wars in the end times. Storms, famines, and pestilence would stalk. There would be earthquakes and hatred toward His followers. Fear would cause people's hearts to fail (Luke 21:26). Jesus talked about this in Matthew chapter 24, we've seen the proof.

Earthquakes are happening in unusual places. Tornados are descending across parts of the United States where they haven't before. Intense weather systems aren't the only things causing storms of immense magnitude. Mass shootings, higher gas prices, food shortages, skyrocketing costs of living, famines, plagues, pestilence, disease, pandemics, crime and chaos of all kinds are affecting every family.

Something as ordinary as busyness can keep people in a perpetual swirl. Road rage spews with bumper-to-bumper traffic where everyone seems to be in a hurry. Tempers can even flare over something as simple as being late for soccer practice.

The storms of life arrive in many forms. They press against us as events line-up to usher in our Savior's return. Jesus said that storms would come, but they don't have to devastate my house. Or yours, for that matter. Like flashing neon lights, the warning signals are all around us. Shofars blare in the spirit. If God's kids listen to His instructions, disaster can pass over as surely as it did for the Israelites when the plagues hit Egypt.

We know they're coming but we don't have to panic. We don't have to holler, bellyache, or fret. God knows how to take care of the birds and He knows how to care for us (Matthew 24:6).

If you want to understand how to protect your family from today's storms and from those to come, this book is for you. Faith alone won't stop the storms that approach our doorsteps. It requires the Word of the Lord and obedience to His voice. According to Melanie, "You can't use your faith to disobey God. Surviving the storms is about obedience, not faith, ego and pride."

We can't lean to our own understanding and expect supernatural results. We're to give up on our own opinions and allow Holy Spirit to lead us. He'll remove the limits of our understanding.

CHAPTER 2

The Shaping of You

The world tries to manipulate us as surely as a puppeteer controls a marionette. There are puppeteers in the spiritual realm that would like to dominate people's thinking and eliminate our free will.

Pied Pipers pop up everywhere. Attempting to lead the blind and naïve, they impersonate the original rat catcher. Tooting hypnotic horns they draw people into a fantasy land. They want to influence our children's morals. Their goal is to ensure that future generations won't be problematic for the new political, social, and religious agendas lying in wait.

Some people don't believe in One God or that we need Him. Others think He's just a crutch for those who need support in life.

I'm reminded of the story about a scientist's encounter with God. As a graduate of one of America's finest universities, he felt confident to approach the God who'd created the galaxies. The God who'd set the boundaries of earth's waters, and the One Who had created him.

God listened patiently as the scientist explained that He was no longer needed. Man had arrived and his primitive need for a God was null and void.

"Man has risen from the depths of an uncivilized, unintelligent, neanderthal caveman. We can travel through space. We can mold and manipulate atoms and genes to transform human anatomy. Not only can we clone life, but we can also create life like You did in the beginning with Adam and Eve."

"That's interesting," God said. "Show me how you do that."

"No problem." The scientist picked up a handful of dirt and began to shape it.

"Oh no," God said, shaking His head. "That's mine. I created that. Get your own dirt."

WE NEED GOD

God created the body of man from the dirt of the earth. However, like God, man's spirit is eternal. Man's physical body will return to dust when our spirit, the life force within leaves (Ecclesiastes 12:7). In the meantime, globalists, researchers, and others who once were invisible influencers are trying to shape our opinion and perspective to further their cause and agenda. When anyone advocates for a system of beliefs and behaviors that contradict God's Truth, the result are storms.

Television and radio talk show hosts are some of them. News networks. Pharmaceutical companies. Cereal manufacturers. Celebrities. Men who use their power to influence your character and purchasing power. Democrats. The Republican party. Every religion of the world is trying to indoctrinate you into their way of thinking, believing, and doing. The list goes on and on.

God is no stranger to man's attempts to cross boundaries and gain the power to be like Him. Adam and Eve wanted to be like God. Satan, the original puppeteer deceived them into sin by acting on their desire. Instead of acknowledging that God created them in His very own image (Genesis 1:27) and that they were already like their Father, they chose their own way of thinking and doing. Instead of remaining obedient to what God said (Genesis 3:5) Satan lured them away.

Not doing things God's way brought an almost never-ending storm into the world. Yes, God is love and full of mercy. That's why God tells us what brings death and destruction into our lives and what will cause the storms to pass over.

LISTENING TO GOD

Many have an aversion to the idea of obedience. Obedience challenges our independence and often irritates our pride. Dictators use force, intimidation and fraud to coerce obedience to their will and agenda. Their goal is to take away our freedoms as they enforce their leadership and power over us. That kind of obedience is never healthy.

Obediencc to God doesn't cause mental or physical anguish or harm, though. It results only in life. "But seek (aim at and strive after) first of all His kingdom and His righteousness (His way of doing and being right), and then all these things taken together will be given you besides" (Matthew 6:33 AMPC).

When the disciples asked what the sign of His return would be, "…Jesus answered and said to them: 'Take heed that no one deceives you'" (Matthew 24:4). Jesus said that many would come in His Name declaring they are the Christ.

Jesus is Christ's Name. Christ is His title and means the Anointed One. Jesus is God's Anointed One. God's grace and truth came by means of Jesus (John 1:17). Jesus Christ is God's Way (John 14:6). Any way other than God's way is deception.

Jesus said, "For nation will rise against nation, and kingdom against kingdom. And there will be famines, pestilences, and earthquakes in various places. All these are the beginning of sorrows" (Matthew 24:7-8). Some translations refer to sorrows as the beginning of birth pains and intolerable anguish (AMPC).

Jesus tells us that the storms are coming.

All of God's creation, as well as each of us, have suffered since sin entered the world. God's creation isn't just tired, it's groaning in pain (Romans 8:22). Ask any woman who's been in labor. Birth pains increase and intensify toward the end. But birth pains don't last forever.

God's creation groans because of evil in the world. Storms are everywhere as nature lashes out. Disaster, pain, turmoil and animal attacks are on the rise. Destruction looms as we do our best to navigate stormy times.

Darkness despises what's good, families are riddled with divorce, incest, and loss of life. Children rebel against authority and many love pleasure more than they love God and one another. Entitlement instead of thankfulness permeates hearts. Evil is called good. People are confused even about the difference between right and wrong.

God's original plan for the earth never included massive tornadoes, tsunamis, or earthquakes. Lions and wolves were intended to lay with the lambs (Isaiah 11:6). God never intended for man to experience hardship or death. God's plan for mankind was only good (Genesis 1).

PERSPECTIVE

You and I are the only ones who can determine what we allow to influence us. Our deepest beliefs are formed by where we focus our time and attention. What we choose to believe and are obedient to by submitting our thoughts and behaviors can create many storms in our lives.

Many people bandwagon specific causes and mindsets. They may even try to instill fear or guilt against those who don't get on board with the trend. For example, when I hear the phrase climate change, my perspective takes me to Genesis, the book of beginnings. "While the earth remains, seedtime and harvest, cold and heat, summer and winter, day and night shall not cease" (Genesis 8:22 AMPC).

I also remember what the Apostle Paul said in the Book of Romans. "For we know that all creation has been groaning

as in pains of childbirth right up to the present time"
(Romans 8:22 NLT).

Does climate change appear to be a real thing? Yes. But we
can allow God to reveal what He has to say about it. God
wants to shape our perspective so that we can be stronger
than the storms that are on the horizon. Stronger than the
potential storms blamed on climate change that may spawn.
Jesus said it like this when He called Matthew to
follow Him.

"And as He was passing by, He saw Levi (Matthew) son of
Alphaeus sitting at the tax office, and He said to him, Follow
Me! [Be joined to Me as a disciple, side with My party!]"
(Matthew 2:14 AMPC). In other words, Jesus invited
Matthew to become part of His way of seeking truth and
being right.

Jesus offers us the same opportunity He gave Matthew.
When we side with Him as His disciples, we can do what He
tells us to do and stand stronger than the storms. We understand that our only confidence is in God. We don't have to
be arrogant or cocky. We don't survive because we pray
better than those who fall victim to the storms. It isn't about
intelligence. We know that the smartest thing we can do is
side with Jesus and let God's Word guide our lives.

When God was delivering the children of Israel from Egypt
and they listened and obeyed, they saw the salvation of the
Lord. When they refused to listen and obey it cost them the
Promised Land (Deuteronomy 1:1-4:43).

Taking God up on His Word requires faith. *My* faith is about me. It's about me, me, my, my and *my* faith, which can be misplaced, weak and even fail when I need it the most.

We can however put our faith and trust in God through His Word. It's only His Word that never fails. Taking God at His Word means we'll have to stand strong on what He says. If you read my book *Never Meet the Devil Naked*, you know why you need a strong spiritual core to support a strong stand. If you haven't read the book, I recommend it.

GOD'S WORD

Isaiah 55:11 is God's promise concerning His Word and where we get our backbone to stand strong against whatever storm arises. "So shall My word be that goes forth out of My mouth: it shall not return to Me void [without producing any effect, useless], but it shall accomplish that which I please and purpose, and it shall prosper in the thing for which I sent it" (AMPC).

I trust God to watch over His Word. That's why I put God's Word between me and my family and whatever storm threatens.

CHAPTER 3

Storm Savvy

Jesus had a knack for taking a simple illustration and using it to teach profound truths. Let's put a Jesus twist on a familiar childhood story.

Remember the three little pigs? The original story dates to the 1800's, but the theme was Biblical long before then. There are several versions, and morals taught with the story. One is that hard work and diligence will pay off in the end.

Three little pigs went out into the world to build prosperous and productive lives. These little pigs were fresh off the farm. One little pig built the house of his dreams with straw, and another built his with sticks. The third little pig built his house with bricks. Each pig became an entrepreneur within the building trades.

Opportunities abounded. Money was easy and life was good. All was going well until one dark and eerie night. Unexpected trouble was the nature of the world in which they lived. Mom, bless her heart, did her best to shelter them from the storms that came along with living life.

The three little pigs' storm came in the form of a very big, very bad wolf that had a hankering for some of those tender, fall-off-the bone ribs. The wolf came calling one brisk October night. He was looking for an open door and a little pig to steal.

"Little pig, little pig, I have a deal for you," the big, bad wolf said.

The first little pig nicknamed Porky, answered, "No, no, I know better than to take your shifty deal. Mama taught her piglets to never let a stranger through the door."

The wolf answered with a promise. One they didn't want to believe. "Then I'll huff, and I'll puff, and I'll blow on your house until all four walls cave in."

Porky tried to get out of there, but he didn't make it. His brother, Jimmy, didn't fare well either. They both ended up in the BBQ pit. The big bad wolf found them very tasty.

The third little pig was the wisest of the three. He'd taken the time to build his house according to the instructions. Instead of straw and sticks, he used bricks laid upon a rock foundation. When wolf roared, the wisdom he'd used saved his bacon.

LIONS, WOLVES AND GOD ALMIGHTY

We have an adversary too. Our enemy prefers lamb chops over little pigs. God tells us that unlike the big bad wolf in our fairy tale story, the devil is real.

"Be sober, be vigilant, because your adversary the devil walks about like a roaring lion, seeking whom he may devour" (1 Peter 5:8). Like a lion, the devil looks for someone to devour. He sends storms and does a lot of huffing, puffing and roaring in hopes of destroying God's lambs.

Jesus said, "'Behold, I give you the authority to trample on serpents and scorpions, and over all the power of the enemy, and nothing shall by any means hurt you'" (Luke 10:19).

God's promise is that nothing will harm us.

Through Jesus Christ, God provided us with an arsenal of personal protection equipment (PPE) that can deliver us from any dark days ahead. God's PPE are found in His Word. They're instructions He gave us to follow so that the storms of life can pass over. God's promises are mighty weapons against the enemy's attacks and strategies. When we follow the instructions, they won't fail us. Therefore, nothing by any means shall harm us.

STORMS

It doesn't have to be a dark and eerie October night. When trouble does come, the question everyone asks is, "What are we going to do now?"

God's prophet, Elisha, was asked that very question.

The king of Syria wasn't happy that God's people were always tipped-off about his strategies to destroy them. Elisha heard from God and was warning Israel's king. When the king of Syria discovered it was Elisha who warned God's people of his plans to storm them, he sent an army by night to seize him.

The next morning when Elisha's servant saw the Syrian army with many horses and chariots he asked the man of God, "…'Alas, my master! What shall we do?' [Elisha] answered, Fear not; for those with us are more than those with them. Then Elisha prayed, Lord, I pray You, open his eyes that he may see…" (2 Kings 6:15-7 AMPC).

The Lord opened his servant's eyes. He could see horses of fire and chariots of fire everywhere upon the mountain (17).

The first thing Elisha said to his servant was stop the fear! As Elisha prayed for his servant's spiritual eyes to be opened, we can ask God to open our eyes that we may see His protection from the danger and storms headed our direction or that are surrounding us. But we must stop the fear.

TRUST GOD

Fear and storms didn't exist in the beginning before Adam and Eve sinned. Fear and storms came when Satan, the god of this world took over. "In whom the god of this world hath blinded the minds of them which believe not, lest the light of the glorious gospel of Christ, who is the image of God, should shine unto them (2 Corinthians 4:4 KJV).

"The god of this world," is the same devil that roams around like a lion looking for someone to devour. He has a blinding effect on those who don't believe what God says— Christian and non-Christians alike. Not to worry though, Jesus overcame him. Throughout the Bible we're guided on how to overcome the storms that are in the world. We must trust God and stop the fear.

"I have told you these things, so that in Me you may have [perfect] peace and confidence. In the world you have tribulation *and* trials *and* distress *and* frustration; but be of good cheer [take courage; be confident, certain, undaunted]! For I have overcome the world. [I have deprived it of power to harm you and have conquered it for you.]" (John 16:33 AMPC).

JESUS IS GOD'S PROVISION

Jesus defeated the god of this world—the devil. The Bible calls Satan a murderer and a liar (John 8:44). God doesn't want us ignorant of his wiles. That's why He informs us about our enemy's nature, his tactics, and the schemes he uses as he attempts to destroy us. Satan's agenda is to devour our lives. We don't have to fall victim and we won't when we understand how to win.

The devil who causes many of the storms we encounter is also called the prince and power of the air (Ephesians 2:2). He won't be locked away until Jesus returns. That's when the birth pains stop. But Jesus went to the cross to deliver us from the enemy's power (Colossians 1:12-13). Receiving what Jesus died to give requires faith and obedience to God's instructions in His Word and through Holy Spirit.

Jesus conquered Satan by His obedience on the Cross and deprived the enemy of his power to harm us. "[God] disarmed the principalities and powers that were ranged against us and made a bold display *and* public example of them, in triumphing over them in Him *and* in it [the cross]" (Colossians 2:15 AMPC).

Through the cross, Jesus Christ was victorious over the principalities of darkness that wage war against us. He stripped the devil of authority over mankind and gave us gifts (Ephesians 4:8) so we can overcome in this life. He teaches us how to be stronger than the storms. Jesus provided us with far more than entrance into heaven.

Satan has been deceiving mankind since our creation, beginning with Adam and Eve (Revelation 12:9). He doesn't want people to know that we have authority over him, his works, and the storms of life. He doesn't want us to know about God's gifts, or what He says in His Word. Satan wants to keep people in fear. Understanding God's truth is crucial if we want the pitfalls of Satan to fail.

IN JESUS

Jesus knew that because we live in the world, we'd face storms.

The COVID-19 storm has been described as a living hell. The pandemic haunted the country. Like the devil, the virus roamed the world seeking to devour people. Sickness and disease cause storms in our lives. In the world we face political storms as people fight for power and control. Our freedoms are attacked. High prices and inflation create financial storms. None of us are unfamiliar with the natural catastrophes that wreak havoc in the world. Sometimes troubles, trials, and frustration seem to appear in every direction at once. We've all experienced some not-so-good stuff. We understand storms come.

The Bible tells us how to defeat Satan, the author of the curse and the bringer of storms.

"And they overcame him by the blood of the Lamb, and by the word of their testimony; and they loved not their lives unto the death" (Revelation 12:11 **KJV**).

Don't let *unto the death* trouble you. It means we're willing to take God at His Word come hell or high water. In my neck of the woods, that also includes high tornadic winds.

Jesus said, "These things I have spoken to you, that in Me you may have peace. In the world you will have tribulation; but be of good cheer, I have overcome the world" (John 16:33).

Although there may be trouble in the world, in Christ, we can have peace. There's no peace when we can't pay our expenses, feed our families or when we suffer from disease or nature's wrath. Those things are all part of the curse that Jesus redeemed us from (Galatians 3:13-14). The curse was never God's will for man. That's why He sent Jesus.

STORMS WILL COME

While we can't avoid all the difficulties that come, for those of us who are "in Him," we can emerge standing. Jesus says there's more to surviving the storms, than having faith. It's not enough to be saved or what's called born-again. Jesus said, "If you live in Me [abide vitally united to Me] and My words remain in you *and* continue to live in your hearts, ask whatever you will, and it shall be done for you" (John 15:7 AMPC).

Jesus said, "If you live in Me." The King James Version renders it, "If you abide in me." That'd be great if Jesus would have stopped there, but He didn't. He went on to say, "And My words remain in you and continue to live in your hearts."

That's what we need to catch. Jesus said a victorious life is determined by how His words live in us. "Therefore, if the Son makes you free, you shall be free indeed" (John 8:36).

PEACE

God's peace is a gift reserved for His kids and is part of His PPE action plan. Peace is one of God's great and precious promises, but it's not automatic.

"Peace, I leave with you, My peace I give to you; not as the world gives do I give to you. Let not your heart be troubled, neither let it be afraid" (John 14:27).

According to that Scripture, we have a responsibility in receiving God's peace. We can't let our hearts be troubled or afraid. It's our choice. We have to stop the fear and focus on God's promises in His Word. That's one way we bring the Word into our hearts and allow God's promises to live in us. We don't have to settle for the world's kind of tranquility when we can have the kind God offers.

Jesus didn't look to the world, science, or the government for answers. He looked to God. Jesus took God up on His promises of peace, provision, and protection. We never see

Jesus fret over what to do. Even now Jesus isn't wound tight over what's going on in the world today. He knew every kind of storm that would knock on our doors. That included pandemics as much as it did the discord over the 2020 election results.

Jesus knew there'd be protests in the streets. He knew the Ukraine's freedom would come under assault. He knew storms would rage over abortion laws, gun regulations, government overreach and racial injustice. Jesus knew about the exploitation of children and the elderly. That's why He left us His peace, His Word and His authority. They're spiritual weapons we employ to put a stop to evil through the power of God. We need these weapons to be stronger than the storms.

As God's kids we must first understand how to stop those storms in our own lives. We have to learn how to stand strong in our own neck of the woods and stop the storms from creeping across the threshold of our lives. In the Lord's prayer, Jesus instructed us to pray that His will would be done on earth as it is in heaven (Matthew 6:10). There are no storms in Heaven.

Terrible things that happen on the earth are not God's will. We also know there are things in our own lives that are not God's will. In heaven, God's will of perfect peace prevails. If having God's will in our individual lives here on earth wasn't possible, Jesus wouldn't have told us to pray that way. While the people in the world may not experience God's will or His peace, those of us who are in Jesus, can.

Yet in the lives of both Christians and non-Christian's alike, people are hurting, suffering and have no peace. Many ask, "Does God care about us? Did He cause this suffering?"

TONI'S TAKE

There was a time when I wondered where God was in the midst of my suffering. I didn't know I had the same opportunity that Jesus offered Matthew, when He said "Come, follow Me and side with My ways."

I wasn't siding with God's ways. I didn't even know He had ways to side with. My life was a mess from abuse, oppression, and my own poor choices. I wondered if God even knew what was going on with me. I questioned, that if He did know, why He wasn't helping me.

I believed in God. I knew He was out there somewhere. Except why was He so silent and difficult to find when I needed answers? Maybe you have some of the same questions I had. Maybe you'd like to know where God is when your life gets tough and stormy.

God gave me the answer many need to hear today. His answer was an understanding about Jesus and how the kingdom of God works. God taught me about the teachings of Jesus, and His PPE promises that He gave to all His kids. Through His Word and Holy Spirit, He gave me an understanding about the storms of life. He opened my eyes to His ways and gave me the wisdom to know that what we're encountering in the world today is a battle between Light and darkness.

I was broken, empty and faced a grim reality—I was out of hope. I wasn't enough to survive the storms I'd encountered in life. I wasn't enough to combat what the devil threw at me. I operated in my own strength and determination which wasn't enough to thrive on the other side of the storms let alone survive the storms. Maybe you feel this way too. There's hope.

I discovered that my relationship with Him through His Word, the Bible, is what influenced the results I experienced in life. Was I valuing and honoring what He said, or trampling what He said as if His Words had no significance to me?

I learned how to have a relationship with God and make choices based on His Word. He showed me how to make His Protection Promise Equipment mine.

I was desperate for a do-over, a new beginning for a life worth living. Maybe you are too. You want a second—or a fiftieth—shot at a good life. Regardless of how you got where you are or how many mistakes you've made or how many times you've picked up the pieces, with God you can build again and better this time.

Maybe you're frustrated and you need to see some progress. You've had enough hard stuff and want to see the results in life that God promised. You're desperate to get out of the rut of taking one step forward, two steps back. I get it. I had to learn how to have the abundant life Jesus promised instead of scraping bottom all the time.

God helped me out of the pit I'd lived in for many years. On the other side of the pit, I had a life to rebuild. This time I built my life on the teachings of Jesus and God's PPE promises. By selecting the right building blocks, God gave me a fresh start in life. God's promises have enabled me to rise above the inevitable storms, which included a pandemic. By following the teachings of Jesus, I overcame the obstacles and built a life that's stronger than the storms. There have been challenges. There will be challenges in your life as well. But you too can be stronger and more courageous than you've ever dreamed possible.

In the midst of the storms that sweep across the world today, you won't have to be one of the frantic people who wring their hands and wonder, "What am I going to do?"

When we ask, "What are we going to do now?" Jesus's answer is build.

"Therefore, whosoever hears these sayings of Mine, and does them, I will liken him unto a wise man, who built his house on the rock: and the rain descended, the floods came, and the winds blew and beat on that house; and it did not fall, for it was founded on the rock" (Matthew 7:24-25).

Hearing and doing what Jesus says to do is essential for enjoying a life that's stronger than the storms.

CHAPTER 4

Building Strong Basics

M y husband, John, and I have built two homes, so we've learned a lot about the construction process. I needed an understanding of the basics that went into home building, especially since I was only familiar with decorating. I loved the beautiful exteriors of rock and log. Meticulous landscapes and the patios that grace the covers of magazines drew me in. I adored grand floor to ceiling fireplaces and large windows that welcomed the sunshine, as well as well-placed furniture that brought a room to life.

In many ways when we look at someone who has built a strong spiritual life, we don't see the evidence of the storms they overcame. All we see is the decorating and adornments. We hear about the healing they received. We observe the prosperity they seem to enjoy. They drive new cars, live in beautiful homes, take regular vacations and enjoy their work. It seems even their children turned out somewhat perfect.

Like building the home where we'll live, fruitful spiritual lives require effort that doesn't always meet an onlooker's eye. Before the decorating is revealed, the wise builder worked behind the scenes as the architect of her life.

She put in the late nights maintaining a connection with God, her provider and power source. She spent time reviewing God's blueprint and instruction manual. She made sure she hadn't overlooked anything that could compromise the integrity of her build. She had the discipline to show up daily—whether worn out or exhilarated from adventure. She showed up week after week, month after month and year after year. Even though she was tired or had a difficult time shutting her mind off, she went to bed thinking on and meditating God's Word. Nothing stopped her from putting forth the effort required for building strong.

"Meditate upon these things; give thyself wholly to them; that thy profiting may appear to all" (1 Timothy 4:15 KJV).

There's more to the building process than skipping through to enjoying God's promise of abundance. Our spiritual lives go deeper than the abundance and jewelry that adorns us. After the diligence and hard work, the profiting that appears to all is the decor that others see.

OUR GENERAL CONTRACTOR

The general contractor is the person in charge of building a home. He oversees the process and takes responsibility for ensuring everything that's needed is on the job site. God, through our general contractor, Jesus, provided everything we need to build a life that won't crumble when storms come. Everything we need to build strong is found in His blueprint called the Bible.

A firm foundation is critical because the integrity of a structure rests on its base. Likewise, the spiritual lives we build rests on our spiritual foundation. A well-built foundation prevents our homes from collapsing under a heavy load or the pressure of outside forces.

Our foundation scripture, Matthew 7:24-25 says, "**Therefore, whosoever hears these sayings of Mine, and does them**, I will liken him unto a wise man, who built his house on the rock: and the rain descended, the floods came, and the winds blew and beat on that house; and it did not fall, for it was founded on the rock" (emphasis mine).

Jesus called the man in this verse wise. What kept his house from falling when the storm hit? What rewarded this wise man with the attention and affirmation of Jesus?

The answer is three-fold. First, the wise man heard and did what Jesus said to do. He was obedient to God's Word and His way of doing things. It wasn't the man who built any way he wanted to build who survived the storms.

Second, the wise man built on the Rock. He didn't expect anyone to build for him. He put forth the effort and built on his foundation. The Rock, also known as Jesus, is the wise man's foundation. When we follow the blueprint and build on the Rock, we can be sure we've built on the integrity of the Bible. We can trust God's faithfulness knowing that He has more than enough power to back His Word.

It's interesting to note, Jesus didn't say the wise man survived the storms because he knew Him—Jesus—as his Savior. Jesus was specific about why the wise man survived the storm. He said the wise man survived because he *built* on the Rock of his salvation. The wise man wasn't a bystander or just singing, *how sweet it is to know Jesus*. He didn't just have a bumper sticker that read, *honk if you know Jesus*. He did more than warm a seat in church on most Sundays and wear a flashing neon Jesus lapel pin. The wise man put in the effort and *built* on the Rock of his foundation by hearing and doing what Jesus said. The implication is that it takes more than being born-again to survive the storms.

The third part of this answer requires trust. Believing is implied in our foundation Scripture. The wise man heard, and because he believed God, he was obedient to do what he heard.

We must take God at His Word. That's part of what's called faith. When we can't see with our natural eyes or understand with our intellect that what the Bible says is possible, we make the choice to give God the benefit of any doubt. When we choose to trust God as an act of our will, light comes. It's like opening the drapes on a sunny day. Light from the Bible illuminates our understanding. When light comes it expels any shadow of doubt and unbelief. Light guides us through the storms.

HAVE FAITH IN GOD

Here's an example of something Jesus said. His teaching in the Book of Mark is a great place to begin building on your foundation. "And Jesus, replying, said to them, Have faith in

God [constantly]" (Mark 11:22 AMPC). His disciples marveled over the withered fig tree, that He'd spoken to. They were astonished that Jesus could speak to a tree and that it would obey Him. Jesus's answer was, "Have faith in God."

Again, the disciples were flabbergasted over a storm that obeyed what Jesus said (Matthew 8:23-27, Mark 4:35-41, Luke 8:22-25). Jesus's response to what seemed impossible was to have faith in God. Jesus said that all things are possible to those who believe. Jesus still tells us today, "Have faith in God."

Nothing in the natural can stop a raging storm. It takes the Word of God and faith in God.

There's no point doing what Jesus says if we don't believe we can have the results He said we can expect. It's called faith in God. God said the just—those who have been justi-fied by the Blood of Christ—will live by faith (Romans 1:17, Galatians 3:11, Hebrews 10:38, Habakkuk 2:4).

If we're to live by faith, then without faith, we may not fare well. Without faith we may not survive the storms. We're called believers for a reason. We believe what God says. Believing is a vital part of the Christian experience. We believe in a God we've never seen. We trust in a Savior we've never seen. We believe the storm will pass over. Believers believe.

TONI'S TAKE

I've experienced the hostile threats of more than one massive tornado. This time, although I was in the storm

cellar, the twister that seemed to be after me was no different. I learned to watch both the sky and the television when
spring storms threatened. When torrential rains descend
with those twisters, the water that gathers between my
garage and my storm cellar rises to about ankle height.
That's not the case for everyone. Many people have survived
a tornado, only to drown in water that had nowhere to go.

On this day it wasn't raining. Nothing deadened the violent
cracks of the lightening I heard as I watched streaks of light
flash across the northwest sky. A sound like a racing freight
train rumbled through the atmosphere.

The winds got rough. As they pushed me around, I sensed
that the churning funnel which picked up homes and
boxcars like tinker toys, destroying everything in its path,
was moving toward us. Like bristles on a broom, the high
winds swept dirt and debris through the air.

Weather predictors had warned residents of our area that
conditions were prime for tornados. Storm chasers had been
on the hunt all day. John had the storm cellar open, swept
clean of spiders and ready to go. When those smoky
columns dropped from the sky, we knew every second it took
to find shelter mattered.

When John insisted it was time to go underground, I went
without my normal protesting. I didn't like being in the
cellar. It was hot and stuffy. I couldn't see what was going on
outside either. I calmed myself by remembering God's
promises. Surrounding myself with God's peace kept me
from feeling like I was trapped in a small, confined space.

We were underground for only a few short minutes when I heard the rushing wind above. What I heard was the sound of massive wind curling and lowering toward us. Every time I heard what sounded like the wind dropping down, I followed one of the sayings of Jesus. I spoke to the storm like Jesus spoke to the raging sea that tried to swallow His first disciples (Mark 4:35-41).

I addressed the tornado. "In Jesus Name, I command you to stay up there. You cannot drop down on us or our home."

I learned to plead the Blood of Jesus over my family and our property, so I also said, "In the Name of Jesus, I plead the Blood of Jesus over us and our home and our neighbors."

I heard the winds reach a peak, then taper. During the quiet intervals between the rising and falling howls of the wind, I heard the whisper of a helicopter.

Swooshing winds rumbled from above us a few minutes later. Knowing my God promised that no deadly thing shall harm me or my family, I continued taking my authority. Again, I told the tornado to stay up there as I pled the Blood of Jesus. The sounds lifted. This went on several times, and each time when the winds quieted, John and I could hear the faint sound of a helicopter.

My cell phone rang. Surprised I had phone service, I answered. It was my brother calling all the way from Michigan.

His voice was high pitched when he asked, "Where are you?"

"In the storm cellar."

"Good!" he said. "Your house is on the news. There's a tornado above you. It keeps lifting and then lowering back down over your house."

Now I understood what I was hearing. The tornado was listening to me. I told the tornado it couldn't drop down, so it went back up. Because I hadn't told it to leave my area, it stayed there above us.

Experience can be but isn't always the best teacher. I prefer to learn from the Bible. The next time I heard the winds descend, I told the tornado where to go. "In Jesus Name, be gone. Leave my neighborhood. Go back to where you came from. I command that you do no damage to our neighborhood."

This time the tornado left, and in a little while we were able to go back inside our home. A few days later we learned that the tornado had landed in a vacant field a short distance down our road.

Over the years I've had plenty of opportunities to take authority over tornados. I prefer to do so sitting on my sofa in the comfort of my living room, but that's not always the case. When the threat is in my area, I consider it wisdom to go underground. We need protection from the storm and debris it sweeps through the air. I can take my authority from the storm cellar. I don't always have to stand toe to toe with any monster.

The tornado that devastated Moore, in May of 2013, roared through the north end of my town before it traveled to Moore. Since then, I've made it my habit to sit in front of the television and speak to tornados as forecasters see them forming. I don't get them all. The scope of my authority for others and the territory of my spiritual jurisdiction has boundaries. One reason is because other people have a free will. But there are plenty of times I do get to rejoice when a weathercaster or storm chaser scratches their head and says something like, *I don't know what happened to it! It was right there!*

I know what happened to the tornado. It dissipated just like I told it to. I've learned a few things about speaking to tornados. I've learned strategies that give me an edge over the storms.

TRUSTING THE PROCESS

I have lots of storm stories. I've also heard testimonies from people who overcame the storms that threatened their families and homes by following the Lord's three-point building plan of success. Hear what Jesus has to say, obey what He says and have faith in God.

For me, building confidence and faith in God and His promises didn't happen overnight. It took time. Like lumber is needed for building a home, knowledge of what God says is the material required for building a strong spiritual life. While it wasn't my first time to speak to a storm, I had the confidence to speak to the tornado because I'd already read in the Bible that I could do the works that Jesus did. I had years of practice too.

"Most assuredly, I say to you, he who believes in Me, the works that I do he will do also; and greater works than these he will do, because I go to My Father" (John 14:12).

When Jesus says, "most assuredly," He's not fooling around. Jesus assured us with adamant conviction that we can do the works that He did if we'll believe. We'll also do greater works than He did. But not one work will happen unless we act on what He says in faith.

That's another saying of Jesus that we're to build with. Jesus said we should do the works He did while on the earth. Now, it's our choice to believe and to do it. If I'd never read the Bible and taken the time to build faith in what Jesus said, I wouldn't have had the knowledge or confidence to act. Reading the Bible is non-negotiable. We can't believe beyond what we have knowledge of.

"Grace and peace be multiplied to you in **the knowledge** of God and of Jesus our Lord, as His divine power has given to us all things that pertain to life and godliness, **through the knowledge** of Him…" (2 Peter 1:2 emphasis mine).

One definition of grace is God's willingness to use His ability to work on our behalf. I wasn't the best math student in school, but I do know that when it's something good, I'd prefer to have it multiplied to me rather than added. You too?

According to Peter, we grow in grace and truth through the knowledge we have about God and Jesus. We gain knowledge by spending time in the Bible, hearing what the Word says, and doing what the Word says to do in faith. I've learned there are no shortcuts.

PEACE AND PLENTY

The COVID pandemic tried the peace of many. I watched a video a pastor recorded updating his congregation on their church. He said he'd received two letters on the same day. In one letter the sender threatened to leave the church if the pastor didn't require everyone to wear masks. The sender of the other letter said they'd leave the church if he *did* require masks.

Fear of the unknown drives people. They're looking for peace that can only be found in relationship with Jesus Christ, through the knowledge of Him in the Bible.

God has already given—past tense—us all things, not *some* things that pertain to life and godliness, but *all* things. The ability to escape the corruption that's in the world comes through His PPE. The promises He's given to us. God gave us those promises but they're not automatic. We must have knowledge of the promises and act on them. We must do what Jesus said to do.

According to 1 Peter 1:2 that we just read, everything that pertains to life, including the grace and peace to survive storms, tragedy, and pandemics, are multiplied to us through knowledge. God says that His kids die from a lack of knowledge (Hosea 4:6).

Would you like God's multiplied grace and peace to flow into your life? Commit to the three success points and trust the process. Hear what He says and obey Him. Have faith in God. God is faithful Who promised. His abundant life belongs to you—take it!

CHAPTER 5

The Bringer of Storms

I f we're going to build lives that are stronger than the storms, we need knowledge about where storms originate.

When severe weather threatens in Oklahoma, we want to know what our meteorologists know. They've studied the atmospheric conditions for years. They're in close contact with the National Weather Service. We need their knowledge so we can be prepared.

Likewise, spiritual preparation is key. We need to stay in vital union with God. There have been many times when God has warned me of danger or a storm the devil's evildoers were plotting.

You may have experienced similar warnings. While driving home from work you sensed an intense urge to take a route other than your usual. Maybe you were about to buy lettuce at the grocery store. For some reason you had a hesitation and put it back. A few days later you heard about a lettuce recall because of an E. Coli outbreak. The store where you shop pulled all the lettuce from their shelves.

Maybe you were planning a vacation but sensed something wasn't quite right. You changed your plans. Months later you learned that the hotel where you planned to stay, burned to the ground on the weekend you would have been there.

By obeying when we sense the Lord's prompting, we avoid the storm that lurks ahead. That's a good time to remember your God. Give Him a quiet, thank You, or a loud shout-out for His protection.

That doesn't mean everything that pops into your head is a warning. God is a Spirit, and He speaks to us through our spirit. That's why we need to take the time to develop that spiritual relationship. For more information see my book *Never Meet the Devil Naked*.

The world can be a war zone. We can't neglect hearing from God or refuse His gifts and promises and expect His protection.

COACH PAUL

The Apostle Paul knew about storms. He said, "We are troubled on every side, yet not distressed…" (2 Corinthians 4:8 KJV).

Paul was beaten, stoned, and left for dead—to name a few of the troubles he encountered in life. Paul knew what it was like to have a storm beating down on him. In Paul's own words, we have his testimony to God's faithfulness.

"Persecutions, afflictions, which happened to me at Antioch, at Iconium, at Lystra—what persecutions I endured. And out of *them* all the Lord delivered me" (2 Timothy 3:11).

All means all. Paul said that no matter what storm came against him, God delivered him from them all. That includes the thorn that many say God never released from Paul. Paul said God did set him free from the thorn in the flesh (2 Corinthians 12:7) as well as every other storm he encountered. God is trustworthy.

Much of what we know about the devil—the bringer of storms—came by revelation that God gave Paul. Allow me to paraphrase our foundation Scripture, Matthew 7:24-25. When Jesus said that storms would come, He's talking about adversity. When hard knocks threatened to beat us down, our method of escape is obedience to what He says.

When I stood against the tornado that threatened my family and our home, I went to war with that beast according to the Word of God. I called upon God through His Word to deliver us. "Call upon Me in the day of trouble; I will deliver you, and you shall glorify Me" (Psalm 50:15).

I heard what God said, I did what God said and by faith trusted Him to deliver. Had I been silent, God would have helped me pick up the pieces.

JESUS SAID SPEAK

Employing our words is an important building block and saying of Jesus that's also known as the prayer of faith.

"So Jesus answered and said to them, "Have faith in God. For assuredly, I say to you, whoever **says** to this mountain, 'Be removed and be cast into the sea,' and does not doubt in his heart, but believes that those things he **says** will be done, he will have whatever he **says**" (Mark 11:22-23 KJV emphasis mine).

Jesus began with "have faith in God." Then He said to use our words to speak to the mountains in our lives. That's steps one, two and three. Believe, hear what He says and do it. The next verse tells us that Jesus said we're to believe we have what we say when we pray.

"Therefore I say to you, whatever things you ask when you pray, believe that you receive *them*, and you will have *them*" (Mark 11:24 KJV).

Mountains can be obstacles like sickness and disease that try to prevent us from having the abundant life Jesus died to give. Mountains can be storms. Regardless of what comes against us, Jesus is the One who said we could have what we say if we'll believe in our heart and have faith in God.

How am I sure that when I speak to a storm or an obstacle such as high blood pressure, cancer or financial lack that it will obey me? I've taken the time to build and put God's Word in my heart and I believe God is true to His Word.

My faith and trust is in God. He's the One who promised. He's the One who will cause it to happen, not me. In my own strength I don't have that kind of power. I can write this with bold confidence because I've experienced super-natural results in my body and in my life by hearing and

obeying this teaching of Jesus. I know many others who
have as well.

KEEP BUILDING

In Mark 11:24, translators rendered the word *ask*, as *desire* in
the King James Version. If we study the original Greek
word, *aieto* to its root, it means *to make a request, a demand of
something due*[1]. What's due? All that God has promised.
Everything that Jesus died to give belongs to us and we take
it by faith.

We receive everything from God by His grace through our
faith (Ephesians 2:8).

It's like going into the bank and asking the teller for the
money they're holding that belongs to you. You make a
withdrawal on what's already yours when you want it.
Unless you put a demand on that money, it'll stay in the
bank. We don't go into the bank with an arrogant attitude
or with a Glock to request what belongs to us. We don't
demand anything from God arrogantly. He is our Father.
We come as His children knowing He said He withholds no
good thing from us (Psalm 84:11).

We might say something like, "Father, in Jesus Name I'm
asking for the healing for my knee that Jesus provided for me
at the cross. I believe I receive it now, and I thank you for it
in Jesus Name." Then you give God thanks and the glory
that you're healthy and pain free. You continue to be
thankful until you see the manifestation if it wasn't instant.
Whether you see an instant result or not, praise God for
what He did, not for what He's going to do.

In verse 24, in the original Greek, Jesus says the time to put a demand on our request is "when we pray." That's when we're to *believe we've received our request.* God wants us to have this kind of trust and confidence in what He says. He wants us to take Him at His Word. Therefore, we're to believe we receive the manifestation of the Word that we've put a demand on when we pray, not when we see the teller put our request in our hot little hands. We believe when we fill out the withdrawal slip. Those who will believe are the people who will have what they say.

We can take authority over a storm that's happening in our bodies. "Cancer! I command you to leave my body in the Name of Jesus. Be gone, and never return. God said I've been redeemed from the curse of the law. Cancer is a curse." Then keep thanking God.

All healing doesn't manifest in an instant. This is where faith comes in. You trust God that the Word is at work doing its job on the inside of you. Every day keep thanking God for the healing Jesus provided.

Declare your healing scriptures in past tense. First Peter 2:24 is written to us in past tense. The provision is already there, waiting for us to put a demand on it.

"Who Himself bore our sins in His own body on the tree, that we, having died to sins, might live for righteousness—by whose stripes you were healed." Were healed is past tense. This scripture is telling us of what Jesus did for us on the cross. He bore our sins and by the stripes He took we were healed. We come into agreement with what God says because He's watching over His Word to preform it (Jeremiah 1:12). It's God's Word that never returns void (Isaiah 55:11).

If the doctor has you on medication, take the Word at the same time you take your meds. Trust God and keep taking your meds until your doctor takes you off them. Continue declaring the Word keeping it in your mouth and heart and believing. Taking medicine does not stop the Word from working.

RECOGNIZING THE BRINGER OF STORMS

There's an old saying, if it looks like a duck, swims like a duck and quacks like a duck, odds are it's a duck. That's a litmus test for identifying something by observing its characteristics and mode of operation.

A man named Job in the Bible experienced a storm from Satan. "And behold, there came a great [whirlwind] from the desert, and smote the four corners of the house, and it fell upon the young people, and they are dead, and I alone have escaped to tell you" (Job 1:19 AMPC).

The devil huffed and puffed through a tornado and caused the walls of the house to fall on Job's kids, killing them all. Job was distraught. Who wouldn't be? Job thought it was God who'd caused the storm. God was the only supernatural power Job knew about at that time. Most people under the Old Covenant, Job included, lived in ignorance of the devil. I once did, too.

It's said of Satan that he always over plays his hand. He overplayed his hand with Job, and with me. Like Job, for years I didn't know there was a devil influencing my life.

Because the devil magnified his evil against Job, we have his testimony that exposes his mode of operation.

Job didn't have the understanding we have available today. Nor did he have our Jesus covenant. In Job 1:11, we see that Job was in the devil's hand. God didn't put Job there, nor did He sic the devil on Job to destroy him. Both ideas contradict God's character. The misconception that God lifted His hand of protection from Job violates Scripture.

Jesus hadn't come yet so we know that Job's spirit wasn't born-again. He lived in the state of man's fallen nature. We also know that as a man, Job had not attained sinless perfection. Jesus was the only sinless One. Job gave the devil permission into his life. How did that happen?

God blessed Job and put a hedge of protection around him (1:10). Job was still full of fear. That anxiety put holes in his hedge of protection which gave the devil access to torment him. Job's life wasn't destroyed because he wasn't good enough or because of his sin. His own unbelief opened the door to the adversary.

God loved Job, but He didn't override his freedom to choose any more than He did with Adam and Eve. Or that He will with you and me. The enemy put a demand on God's Word of honor and integrity. Satan knew Job was in violation of God's Word because he'd been observing him (Job 1:8). We can see duck tracks all over Job's story. "He who digs a pit shall fall into it, and whoever breaks through a wall will be bitten by a serpent" (Ecclesiastes 10:8).

Our Jesus Covenant makes all the difference for our ability to withstand the storms. When the devil tried to take my house with a tornado, he didn't get away with it. I'd already heard what Jesus said to do in these situations. Job didn't have the knowledge or the authority that Jesus died to give. Like our role model, Jesus, I spoke to the storm. I believed what Jesus taught, I obeyed, and I got the results Jesus got.

If you're one of the people who think God allowed the devil to destroy Job's life—you are deceived and believing a lie of the devil. Believing that lie will create an opening for the devil to operate. He'll whisper words in your ears like, "Why trust God after what He did to Job and Paul?"

The bringer of storms wants to cause doubt in people's minds so that they don't have confidence in God. *Well, if God did it to poor old Job, what's stopping Him from doing it to me?*

The devil knew God was the source of Job's wealth and prosperity. The Bible records Satan's knowledge of God's blessing and protection. Speaking to God, Satan said, "Does Job fear God for nothing? Have You not made a hedge around him, around his household, and around all that he has on every side? You have blessed the work of his hands, and his possessions have increased in the land" (Job 1:10).

Satan knew the source of Job's wealth. He also knew he was in fear and not trusting God (1:5, 3:25).

Spreading lies about Paul and Job are strategies the devil uses against the church. Satan spreads lies against God's nature and character. He doesn't want us to put our trust and faith in Him.

TONI'S TAKE

I'd already pled the Blood of Jesus over my property whether I was home or not. The angels that are encamped around my house have my back. Should the tornado have taken my home, I believe God would have restored far more than I had. He would have turned that storm for my good, like He turned Job's storm for good.

"And the LORD restored Job's losses... Indeed, the LORD gave Job twice as much as he had before" (Job 42:10).

Like Job, many Christians lack understanding about God and the devil. They don't understand the storms they encounter, or why.

That's why we're doing a little storm investigation as we build. Chasing storms is always popular here in Oklahoma, especially during the seasons that spawn tornados.

I always plead the Blood of Jesus and station angels around my family, our vehicles, and homes. "Bless the Lord, you His angels, who excel in strength, who do His word, Heeding the voice of His word" (Psalm 103:20).

Angels listen for and perform God's Word. God gave us His Word in the Bible. That's one reason we need to know what the Bible says and why we need to obey the teachings of Jesus. I take an aggressive approach to winning over the storms. That includes employing my angels. I do what Jesus said to do to the best of my knowledge and I have faith in God. My trust is in Him, not angels.

THE BRINGER OF THE STORM IN EDEN

The Garden of Eden was a paradise that Adam and Eve didn't want to leave. Eden was a perfect environment, void of battles and storms until that duck named Satan, landed, and took the form of a serpent. Adam and Eve had plenty to eat and lots of Sonshine. Think Hawaiian Islands without the high cost of living, volcanos and tourists. All Adam and Eve had to do was trust God's provision to meet their every desire. God wants us to trust Him to meet our every need and desire.

Adam and Eve lived the abundant life God wants all of us to enjoy. But they blew it. Eve was first to eat the forbidden fruit before offering a bite to Adam. Scripture is clear, Eve was deceived, not Adam. It was Adam's sin that brought the fall of man (Romans 5:12,13). Adam created a storm that passed to all his descendants by opening a door to the devil through disobedience. He didn't listen and obey.

The fall was never about the fruit. It was about hearing and doing the one thing that God said. Although it was never God's perfect will for man, we continue to face storms and battles instigated by the same duck. Adam gave Satan permission into the lives of his descendants.

"For we are not wrestling with flesh and blood [contending only with physical opponents], but against the despotisms, against the powers, against [the master spirits who are] the world rulers of this present darkness, against the spirit forces of wickedness in the heavenly (supernatural) sphere" (Ephesians 6:12 AMPC).

Notice that in this translation, the Apostle Paul said we weren't *contending only with physical opponents.* Paul knew the storms we'd encounter in life would be designed by the same enemy that incited the storms he withstood. Paul knew they would be demonic in nature.

Satan often spews his poison through people we know. He may work through someone at your job or school. He may send an unscrupulous contractor that promises to rebuild your home after a storm. You give him the deposit, then never see him again. We can't blame people for the problems in the world or in our individual lives. They may be our problem because they submit to the devil's will, but it's Satan who is behind all evil.

Because of a lack of knowledge, the Bible tells us many people are taken captive by Satan at his will.

"And that they may recover themselves out of the snare of the devil, who are taken captive by him at his will" (2 Timothy 2:26 KJV).

Anyone taken captive by the devil needs our prayer. They've been deceived and most don't even know they're being used. We don't fight people, nor do we use human weapons. Our spiritual weapons are more powerful. Since we can't see or feel many of them, we must train ourselves to trust that God is working on our behalf.

"For the weapons of our warfare are not carnal but mighty in God for pulling down strongholds, casting down arguments and every high thing that exalts itself against the knowledge of God, bringing every thought into captivity to the obedience of Christ" (2 Corinthians 10:4-5).

What are our weapons? Allow me to paraphrase Revelation 12:11. We overcome the devil by the Blood of Jesus, the word of our testimony which is the Word of God and we're not ashamed or embarrassed about how that may look to naysayers. We have God's promises, the Blood of Jesus and His Name, fasting and prayer, worship and praise, hearing and obeying, and Holy Spirit, to name a few of our weapons.

All people, Christians, and non-Christians alike, have the same enemy. Those without Jesus, don't have any weapons to use against Satan. And many who do have Jesus, don't know they have weapons, or understand how to use them. We must learn and do things God's way.

Human weapons and strength are useless against a spiritual adversary. People without God's help are desperate and frustrated. They're looking for help anywhere they can.

"… Woe to the inhabitants of the earth and the sea! For the devil has come down to you, having great wrath, because he knows that he has a short time" (Revelation 12:12).

TONI'S TAKE

Some storms we encounter are self-inflicted like mine were before I found out I could have a relationship with God. That said, the devil was still the instigator of the storms in my life. My decision-making skills were tainted. The devil incited and manipulated many of my choices through other people and propaganda. I suffered from a lack of knowledge about God and the devil. I was as ignorant about the storms in life as the three little pigs were.

CHAPTER 6

Stop the Fear

F ear is both a demonic strategy and a spiritual force. Although the storm named Coronavirus was first identified in Wuhan, China, I believe the devil was behind it. It was a plague inspired by unseen demonic forces.

The god of this world, the devil (2 Corinthians 4:4) influences the opinions and actions of people. He likes to instill fear and control our emotions and our thoughts. I believe he used the virus to further his agenda of stealing, killing and destroying (John 10:10).

Through the pandemic he stole jobs and ruined the businesses of many. People died. Families were torn apart and devastated. Churches and gathering places were closed. Sports were canceled, schools shut down and our way of life seemed threatened. He controlled much of what we saw and heard on television.

During the COVID-19 storm that rocked the nations, the enemy launched a full-scale attack against our livelihoods, relationships and our health. Smiling faces were masked. Children were forbidden on playgrounds and from visiting their grandparents for fear of spreading the virus. Santa events were canceled. People masked-up either out of fear or in cooperation with government mandates. Others refused to wear masks. Instead of burning bras, they wanted mask burning parties.

Instead of turkey it was duck for Thanksgiving and Christmas dinner. We can chase this storm all the way back to Satan. Do you recognize that duck's webbed footprints?

"For God hath not given us the spirit of fear; but of power, and of love, and of a sound mind" (2 Timothy 1:7 KJV).

If Satan has a middle name, it could be chaos. He *is* the spirit of fear, and he causes destruction and chaos. "The thief does not come except to steal, and to kill, and to destroy. I have come that they may have life, and that they may have *it* more abundantly" (John 10:10).

Jesus said He came that we might have abundant life. But the reason the devil comes is only to steal, only to kill and only to destroy us and all we hold dear. Which side of John 10:10 would you place COVID-19?

This duck has a three-fold purpose: stealing, killing, and destroying people's character, identity, and lives. That's the devil's M.O. Whether it's a direct attack as we saw with Job, or by influencing and motivating someone under his control to antagonize like we saw with Paul.

We recognize the devil's activity and influence by the deed. We recognize his duck prints. We hear his quack. Anything that steals from you, attempts to kill you, and conspires to destroy your life, according to Jesus, is evidence of the devil at work. The devil is behind all evil.

You can agree with what Jesus said, or not. Call it bad luck, karma, being in the wrong place at the wrong time. Or you can call it like you see it. The choice of what you believe is always yours to make. You have the choice and the ability to side with what Jesus says even if you don't understand it on an intellectual level. It's called believing what God says by faith.

In my opinion, no matter how we carve that duck, the devil was behind COVID-19. His game plan was based on fear. At the release date of this book, fear is still a factor. The Bible, our blueprint, tells us that Satan is the spirit of fear. Fear, either real or perceived, triggers an intense, alarming sense of urgency, danger, and anxiety. It can cause premature death. Most of us have heard the expression, *scared to death*.

Fear induces chemical reactions and imbalances in the brain that can damage the human body. The spirit of fear has an agenda and when we yield to it, it gives the enemy permission into our lives. The result can be a multitude of health storms within our body. It's no wonder God tells us to stop the fear.

Bible scholars report that there are more than 365 references relating to *do not fear* in the Bible. That's one for every day of the year. To survive, we must listen to God so that we're stronger than the storms that fear creates. "Do not be seized with alarm and struck with fear, little flock, for it is your Father's good pleasure to give you the kingdom!" (Luke 12:32 AMPC).

FEAR'S TALONS

Fear begins in the brain—Satan's battlefield. Once the bait is set in the mind, it causes physical and emotional responses that create many adverse reactions in our bodies. Living under a prolonged threat negatively impacts our mental and physical health, not to mention our relationships.

Fear weakens our immune systems. It increases the heart rate and can damage the cardiovascular system. It shuts down the digestive system and can cause intestinal problems. Alarm increases hormones in the brain area known as the amygdala. The amygdala enables us to focus on a present danger or the potential threat, and then store that information in our memory.

When we feel unsafe and vulnerable because we're living under a threat, our instinct prepares us to fight or flee. The longer we live under a threat the more damage can be done. Outside the gates of paradise, man has gotten up close and personal with lions and tigers and bears. But God offers us His peace.

TONI'S TAKE

Fear of my environment caused me to run away from home from as young as two years old. I didn't stop running until I was five. My fleeing ended when a new fear of stray dogs emerged. I was more terrified of a sharp-toothed, aggressive dog with a deep growl than I was of my mother. I didn't feel safe at home. I didn't feel safe in the world. That left me with nowhere to run. For many years, I felt caged and trapped. Through the Word, I've learned that I don't have to live in bondage to fear. The Word set me free.

Just like COVID-19 damaged our ability to connect with others, fear took root in me and damaged my perception of the world and of myself. I hid behind a mask in the great masquerade called life. Fear altered my perception of life and influenced my choices. Instead of recognizing the real enemy many succumb to it—like Job did. Like I did.

NO FEAR, NO PLAGUE

I'm not saying the coronavirus isn't real. I am saying our outcome can very well depend on what we do with those quacks and whether we entertain fear-filled thoughts. Being stronger than the storms means we must choose to believe what God says over what any quacking duck has to say. In the case of the coronavirus, every time that duck quacks, we should remind ourselves that God said no plague shall come near us. "There shall no evil befall you, nor any plague or calamity come near your tent (Psalm 91:10 AMPC).

That's God's promise. However, it's conditional upon hearing and doing what He says in verses one and two.

"He Who dwells in the secret place of the Most High shall remain stable and fixed under the shadow of the Almighty [Whose power no foe can withstand]. I will say of the Lord, He is my Refuge and my Fortress, my God; on Him I lean and rely, and in Him I [confidently] trust!" (Psalm 91:1-2 AMPC).

We have faith in God as we use our words to agree with Him and declare, *I say of the Lord, He is my Refuge and my Fortress, my God in Whom I trust.* If we want the décor, the testimony and the fruit of Psalm 91, then we continue to trust in Him daily to see us through the storms. We take that position, refuse to change our profession of faith and we dwell there, fixed and unmovable in our trust that God is our Fortress, and we rely on Him.

When we believe in our heart and declare God's promise that no plague shall come near us, we're testifying that Jesus is Lord over the plague. We're building on our Rock.

Where any virus is concerned, we can thank God for His continual protection by saying something like, "Although the virus encompasses me about, I choose to take You at Your Word Father God. No virus and no plague shall befall me or my family. I believe Your Word is at work protecting us. Your Word my Father, and my God, is good enough for me."

When we use our words to agree with God's promise, we're testifying to truth above what anyone or any circumstance have to say. Psalm 103:20, states that angels are watching and listening for God's Word. When we're obedient to speak God's Word, we release the angels promised in Psalm 91:11:

"For He will give His angels [especial] charge over you to accompany *and* defend *and* preserve you in all your ways [of obedience and service]" (AMPC).

That's one reason we can be stronger than the storms that come our way. It's all part of receiving what His grace provides through our faith. "For with the heart one believes unto righteousness, and with the mouth confession is made unto salvation" (Romans 10:10). God's grace is always available. The only thing we have to do with God's grace is to tap it with our faith.

CHAPTER 7

Dwelling and Abiding

We began building with John 15:7 (AMPC) in chapter three. Let's look at this scripture from the New King James Bible. "If you abide in Me, and My words abide in you, you will ask what you desire, and it shall be done for you."

Jesus said His Word must remain (AMPC) or abide in us. Dwelling in the secret place of the Most High means to live there. We don't merely visit when we need a hot meal or a few bucks until payday. The verse says that those who dwell in the secret place will say that God is their Refuge, their Fortress and their God. They will be the ones who have the faith and confidence in Him to say that they lean on, rely on and trust in Him. They will believe that He is. Even in a frightening situation they will trust and have faith in God's Word because they are confident in His faithfulness.

Abiding helps us guard our hearts and minds against becoming fearful. That doesn't mean we ignore the harsh quacks trying to communicate their agenda. I didn't wait for the tornado to hit my house before I headed for shelter or took authority over the storm. I didn't wait for my brother to call. His telephone call gave me insight about what was happening, but I'd already spoken to the tornado. I took measures to protect myself, my family, and our home. Based on the authority of the Word of God, I stood against the threat when I heard the first quack. I put the Word between my family and the storm.

I took measures to protect myself and my family when the CDC released their COVID-19 guidelines. I also did my own research and listened to many doctors. I added supplements to help my body fight-off the virus should it be in my vicinity. I also refused to participate in all the negative talk and get into fear over it. I did what Psalm 91 says to do. "I said of the Lord that He is my Refuge, my Fortress and my God." Present tense. I said it and I believed it with bold confidence in God's faithfulness.

It's automatic for me to function that way because I've renewed my mind to God's Word. I've trained myself so that trusting God comes first. If anything comes that wants to steal, kill or destroy me or my family, I recognize it for the duck that it is. That takes time and discipline. Renewing our minds is a warfare strategy. We need to stay ahead of the storm with God's Word. We need to become skillful about the thoughts we allow into our minds daily, not just when a storm threatens. Rather than thinking fearful thoughts, we must choose to think on God's Word that will empower us on a continual basis.

BUILDING CHOICES

Instead of allowing fear to have its way with me, I chose to believe what God says about any situation. Because I've spent time in the Bible, allowing God's Word to retrain my thinking, I've grown in knowledge and understanding. I know what God says to do when a storm threatens. I've heard what He said, I act on His faithfulness to His Word and chose to believe. I replace fear's lie by speaking words that agree with what God says instead.

Reading the Bible and hearing God's Word will help you grow in knowledge and understanding so that you too can know what to do when any kind of storm threatens. This way of life is available for all of God's kids.

If the thought of severe illness from any sickness, disease or virus was to quack at me, I speak back. "No way, devil! God promised that no plague shall come near me or my household. That's Psalm 91:10 and I claim it in Jesus Name. And God is faithful who has promised."

I've learned to say the same thing against any threat including a cold. I said the same thing when breast cancer threatened. The promises in Psalm 91 were the first protection promises I learned. They're great PPE to begin building a life that's stronger than the storms.

Being stronger than the storm isn't popping off with the right Scripture that makes it a reality. It's a way of life. We allow God's Word to take root and live in us as we put faith and trust in Him. We receive all of God's promises by His grace through the verbal agreement of our faith from our heart, the same way we receive eternal life (Ephesians 2:8-9).

It's not by grace alone and it's not by faith alone. God doesn't fight our battles or quiet the storms without us.

FRIGHTFUL THOUGHTS

We can't come against toxic thoughts with another thought of like kind. If we want to be stronger than the storms, we change the direction of our thinking to agree with what God says. That takes the double-edged sword of God's Word. I've trained myself not to fear by hearing, believing, and acting on Psalm 91. Little by little my words of agreement with what God says replaced the tormenting thoughts.

Fearful or traumatic quacks must be dethroned from our mind. We can't dwell on thoughts that contradict God's Word. Changing from fearful thoughts that darkness offers to thoughts that agree with what God says takes discipline and a decision of our will. It's always wisdom to agree with God by managing our thought life. When we make a habit of feeding on the Word, our thoughts become more like God's thoughts.

Dr. Caroline Leaf is a communication pathologist and cognitive neuroscientist, with a Masters and PhD in Communication Pathology and a BSc Logopaedics, specializing in Cognitive and metacognitive neuropsychology.[1] Dr. Leaf has done extensive research on the brain. She teaches on how such things as fear and trauma, as well as positive thinking that's based on God's Word, affect our health. Dr. Leaf is known for her saying that man has been "wired for love."

"Science and Scripture both show that we are wired for love and optimism and so when we react by thinking negatively and making negative choices, the quality of our thinking suffers, which means the quality of our brain architecture suffers. It is comforting—and challenging—to know that negative thinking is not the norm."[2]

If you're like me, you want your brain functioning at peak performance all the days of your life. When thoughts attempt to bombard my mind with fear or negativity, I choose to replace those thoughts with ones that are optimistic and maintain hope in God's promises. I want a happy, blessed life and a future that's stronger than the storms I'll encounter.

We can't afford to allow thoughts that disagree with what God says to infiltrate our mind. To be strong in the Lord requires reading the Bible as we continue to grow and discover what God has to say, then abide there.

Dr. Leaf says, "There isn't a structure, tissue, cell, protein, molecule, atom, or quantum wave that is designed for toxic thinking; we are wired for love, and we learn to fear."[3]

The behavior of Job's children taught him fear (Job 1:5). He said the thing he "greatly feared" had come upon him (Job 3:25).

Remember what I said earlier—Job did not have our Jesus covenant. Don't allow the enemy to put condemnation on you if you've been in fear about something. The way out of that bondage is to repent. That means to change the direction of how and what you've been thinking and acting on. Ask God to forgive you for entertaining any negative, fear-

filled thoughts. Those thoughts are the result of an unre-
newed mind and are deceptive morsels that the enemy
offers.

Then ask God to help you replace those thoughts with His
thoughts. It's that simple. Anytime fearful or negative
thoughts pop into your head, use your words and lift God's
higher thoughts, such as—Psalm 91:10—above them.

Words are the product of thoughts. When we feed on God's
Word, we have His higher thoughts in us. Our words are
thought containers.

AN EXAMPLE

Maybe you have concerns about your children. I've had
concerns over mine. I made it my habit to speak Jeremiah
1:5 and 29:11, over them and any negative thought that
popped into my head about them. I've left it to you to look
up those scriptures. That's you building on your
foundation.

If you have fearful thoughts, declare that God has not given
you the spirit of fear. I've had to speak that promise many
times. I also refuse to touch fearful things with my tongue.
By reading God's Word I've learned that God said, "Death
and life *are* in the power of the tongue, And those who love
it will eat its fruit" (Proverbs 18:21).

We can't let our thoughts become words that produce death.

Today, when anxiety attempts to bombard my mind, I say,
"No way devil. I refuse to fear. God has not given me the
spirit of fear but of love and of power and a sound mind."

That's part of 2 Timothy 1:7 (KJV). Look it up in your Bible and start building.

If I had concerns over getting dementia or Alzheimer's, that's the Word of the Lord I'd start building with.

STRESS

I've been in meetings where I've had the pleasure of hearing Dr. Leaf speak. I've also read several of her books. As a researcher and student of the Bible, I concur with Dr. Leaf. Scientific thought backs up the Bible. "We are constantly reacting to circumstances and events, and as this cycle goes on, our brains become shaped by the process in either a positive, good-quality-of-life direction or a negative, toxic, poor-quality-of-life direction. So, it is the quality of our thinking and choices (consciousness) and our reactions that determine our "brain architecture"—the shape or design of the brain and *resultant* quality of the health of our minds and bodies."[4]

Dr. Leaf says, "Toxic thinking wears down the brain."[5]

I've experienced the effects of how thoughts that are contrary to what God says, wear me down. Maybe you have too.

I've had years of experience recognizing negative thoughts when they come. But they still come. I have to stay on top of them when they do. When a lie—anything that contradicts God's Truth, comes into my head, begins dictating my behavior and emotions, I know I've allowed it access and given it a place in my thinking. When that happens, instead of fighting a thought, I have to fight to stop what that thought is attempting to build and prevent it from rooting deeper. A thought that's been allowed to take root is called a stronghold. We don't want to allow anything contrary to what God says to erect a stronghold in our minds. We need to nip them in the bud when they first show up so they don't become a problem.

Dr. Leaf says, "Research shows that *DNA actually changes shape according to our thoughts*. As you think those negative thoughts about the future—the week ahead, what a person might say or do, even in the absence of the concrete stimulus—that toxic thinking will change your brain wiring in a negative direction and throw your mind and body into stress."[6]

One dictionary defines stress as a "constraining force or influence: such as: a physical, chemical, or emotional factor that causes bodily or mental tension and may be a factor in disease causation."[7]

Many things in life cause stress. Toxic stress creates storms. Disease and fear are two of them. Stress is our body's response to something that requires our attention or our need to act. Dr. Leaf says that some of the stress we experience is normal.

"Stress stage one is normal. This is our alert state that keeps us focused and conscious and is the state we are in when we are thinking in alignment with God. Stress stage two and stage three, however, are our mind and body's response to toxic thinking—normal stress gone wrong."[8]

I work at maintaining a normal stress level. You may have to, also.

God wants us to live life trusting Him, in a peaceful state of existence. Spending time in the Bible has helped me eliminate stress and achieve a higher quality of life. I enjoy greater levels of God's peace today, than I have in the past.

By taking God's promises, His PPE that are written in the Bible, I've experienced abundant life. His promises help me live in perfect peace, root out fear and be stronger than the storms so that I live in harmony with Him. They will help you too.

NO CURSE

Galatians 3:13-14 declares that Christ has redeemed us from the curse. The curse comes to steal, kill and destroy. It includes spiritual death, sickness and disease, lack and poverty. Disease and poverty are storms, not the abundant life Jesus died to give. Unless we spend time reading our Bible, we won't know that the curse has no right to operate in our lives. We won't understand about God's PPE, or any of the benefits that Jesus died to give.

If we've been redeemed from the curse of sickness and disease—and we have been—we're not supposed to die as a result of any sickness or disease. When we've run our race here on the earth and are ready to go to Heaven, we should just close our eyes, go to sleep, and wake-up in Heaven. What's to fear?

BLESSED PEACE

About man, God says, "For as he thinks in his heart, so *is* he…" (Proverbs 23:7).

What have you been thinking about? Are you allowing toxic thoughts to have free reign in your mind? Do you live in the peace and joy Jesus died to give you?

A practical building step toward peace is to take one of God's promises about peace and thank Him for it by turning it into your profession of faith like the one below. Here are a few others for you to look up: John 14:27, John 16:33 and 2 Peter 1:2.

"Father, I see in Your Word that in Christ, You've made your peace available to me. You said I didn't have to live in fear or dread or unrest as the world lives. Thank You for Your peace. I believe I receive Your peace now." Then just sit in His Presence with a grateful and thankful heart. Let God show Himself strong in your life. Every time fear tries to overcome you, repeat the process. Soon, God's promises will become rooted deep within your heart. The faith and confidence produced by God's Word will rise on the inside of you like a volcano whenever you need it. That's the force of faith that operates from within. And yes, you can sense it.

CHAPTER 8

The Training Ground of Hearing and Obeying

The devil has deceived many in the church into thinking all they need is to be saved and everything will work out. Once saved, God will fight all their battles for them. If things don't work out, then it must not have been God's will.

From our foundation Scripture, God fighting our battles or chasing the storms away for us is not the message that Jesus taught. Jesus said we need to build on the Rock. He didn't say God would build for us. Having Jesus as our strong foundation is only the beginning. The more we build, the less vulnerable we become. Let's revisit our foundation Scripture.

"Therefore, whosoever hears these sayings of Mine, and does them, I will liken him unto a wise man who built his house on the rock: and the rain descended, the floods came, and the winds blew and beat on that house; and it did not fall, for it was founded on the rock" (Matthew 7:24-25, emphasis mine).

HIS WORD IN US

Jesus said, "If you live in Me [abide vitally united to Me] and My words remain in you *and* continue to live in your hearts, ask whatever you will, and it shall be done for you" (John 15:7 AMCP).

This Scripture reveals far more than a basis for a prayer request. Let's pause and selah Jesus's instructions for a minute. Selah means to pause, take a moment, and think deep about what you've just heard while reading the Word.

In the New King James Version, this verse reads: "If you abide in Me, and My words abide in you, you will ask what you desire, and it shall be done for you."

Jesus said that His words must live, remain, and continue in us—that's a qualifier. It means this PPE promise is conditional to His Words living in us.

For His Word to be in our hearts, we have to put His Word in there by building. One way we do that is through the power of our imagination. As we begin seeing ourselves based on how God sees us, the Word reveals our God identity and awakens our hidden potential. That's when lasting change happens, and we move into the realm of a whole and abundant life.

Joshua is one example where Scripture gives us the opportunity to witness how our God potential blooms through the imagination. Joshua followed in Moses' sandals. He was there when Moses commanded the people with God's Word and through their obedience to do what He said, the death angel passed over their homes in the Land of Goshen. They applied the three steps that Jesus teaches. First, they heard what God said. Second, they did what God said. Third they believed God.

WARRIOR SUCCESS

Joshua was a warrior. When he took over for Moses, God told him the secret to successful leadership and fulfilling his God potential.

"This Book of the Law shall not depart from your mouth, but you shall meditate in it day and night, that you may observe to do according to all that is written in it. For then you will make your way prosperous, and then you will have good success" (Joshua 1:8).

Joshua didn't have the entire Bible like we have today. He had the first five books of the Hebrew Bible known as the Torah that were written by Moses.

Joshua had God's Word in both written form and spoken— what God spoke to him orally. All of God's Word, the entire Bible was first spoken by God before it was written. God's spoken Word carried His thoughts that became reality.

"For I know the thoughts that I think toward you, says the LORD, thoughts of peace and not of evil, to give you a future and a hope" (Jeremiah 29:11).

God told Joshua, get My Word in your mouth and meditate on My Word day and night. Before he could do that Joshua had to have God's Word in his thoughts. That's God's way. He thinks first then He speaks words.

It's important to note here that God never said He would fight Joshua's battles for him. God said that Joshua would make his own way prosperous and successful by keeping His Word at the forefront of his thoughts and speech. Meditation allows our imaginations an opportunity to change our thinking and see a new and better result than what may have plagued our minds.

God wanted Joshua prosperous and successful. That's why He told Joshua the success principle that would elevate him in battle and in life. God told Joshua how to be stronger than the giant storms heading his way. God also wants you and me to survive every battle or storm, every time, or He wouldn't have told us how. That's success. God helps us as we build with His weapon, the Word.

"For the word of God is quick, and powerful, and sharper than any two-edged sword, piercing even to the dividing asunder of soul and spirit, and of the joints and marrow, and is a discerner of the thoughts and intents of the heart" (Hebrews 4:12 KJV).

Let's look at Joshua 1:8 from the Amplified Bible.

"This Book of the Law shall not depart out of your mouth, but you shall meditate on it day and night, that you may observe *and* do according to all that is written in it. For then you shall make your way prosperous, and then you shall deal wisely *and* have good success."

God told Joshua to meditate in His Word day and night and not to let it depart from his mouth. Why? So that he would observe to do all the Word said to do. That's steps one and two from our foundation scripture. Through obedience to

God's Word, Joshua would make his way, "prosperous…deal wisely and have good success."

This sounds a lot like Jesus saying that the wise man who will hear and do what He says will survive the storms. Surviving the storms and thriving on the other side of them is success.

By meditating and keeping God's Word in his mouth, Joshua was a wise builder. He prospered and had good success just like God promised. Joshua was stronger than the giant storms that he faced in life.

There's a connection between meditating and using our imagination. Both involve engaging our thoughts. Christian meditation means that we think about, ponder, and mutter God's Word. We fill our minds with God's PPE promises. We acknowledge God as God, through thanksgiving and praise.

Participants in Eastern meditation empty their minds. As Christians, we allow God's Word to have the throne in our thought lives.

STORMS

Joshua led the Israelites as they took possession of the Promised Land. God prepared him for the giants he'd encounter by telling him to think, speak and do His Word. By speaking the Word of God, Joshua shifted the focus of his imagination from his giant problem to victory. His thoughts became the solution he uttered with his words. Joshua was obedient to hear and obey. Obedience made

Joshua stronger and more courageous than a thousand giants. Look at the next verse.

God said, "Have I not commanded you? Be strong and of good courage; do not be afraid, nor be dismayed, for the Lord your God *is* with you wherever you go" (Joshua 1:9).

Joshua may have considered the giants and possible outcomes of that storm. He may have been apprehensive about becoming the new leader. Filling Moses' sandals was a tall order. It's reasonable to believe that the more Joshua obeyed, the more he believed and the more courageous he became. That's how God's Word works in us, too. Hear, believe, and do.

STRENGTH FOR ALL THINGS

Being strong and courageous is a requirement to over-coming the storms. We must do as God instructed Joshua. Let me offer my paraphrase of Joshua 1:8: My Word must be in your mouth at all times. Think about my Word and talk up My Word because as you hear it, it will grow faith in you for the impossible. If you'll do this, then you'll make your way prosperous and then you'll have good success.

In chapter four we discussed the saying of Jesus that's also referred to as the prayer of faith.

Jesus said, "For assuredly, I **say** to you, whoever **says** to this mountain, 'Be removed and be cast into the sea,' and does not doubt in his heart, but believes that those things he **says** will be done, he will have whatever he **says**" (Mark 11:23 emphasis mine).

These words came from the mouth of Jesus. He operated in this success principle. We see the evidence throughout the Gospels. Jesus is the One who said we could have what we say, when we believe what we say in our heart. I've learned what I'm believing and saying must line up with the Word of God. Each of us will choose whether we agree with Jesus or not. How we receive and think about the things of God can propel us or hold us back.

To recap what God said about man: "For as he thinks in his heart, so is he..." (Proverbs 23:7)

The heart referred to in this verse is not the organ that pumps blood. That heart can't think. The heart in these verses is our spirit where the kingdom of God is located (for more information see *Never Meet the Devil Naked*). We engage our spirit through our words of agreement with God's Word. Along with activating our imagination through meditating on our God given identity, we build confidence in God and release our potential.

Through the Word of God, we go from spiritual weakness to spiritual strength. On our own, we function as mere men that are no match for the storms or behemoths of life. To realize the potential in this next verse, we must agree with God through our words and meditate on it.

"I have strength for all things in Christ Who empowers me [I am ready for anything and equal to anything through Him Who infuses inner strength into me; I am self-sufficient in Christ's sufficiency]" (Philippians 4:13 AMPC).

God has given us everything we need to be stronger than the storms.

THE WISE WARRIOR

God told Joshua that if he wanted to be successful, he had to engage his thoughts and get his words involved with his outcome. Joshua heard the Word of the Lord and he obeyed. He believed God.

There's no faster way to develop and grow our faith to receive what God promises than to hear our own words agreeing with God's Word (Romans 10:8). We get God's Word in our hearts by hearing it. Then we continue to nurture it by thinking, pondering and speaking it.

The Book of James has a lot to say about that powerful muscle in our mouth called the tongue. "Indeed, we put bits in horses' mouths that they may obey us, and we turn their whole body. Look also at ships: although they are so large and are driven by fierce winds, they are turned by a very small rudder wherever the pilot desires. Even so the tongue is a little member and boasts great things. See how great a forest a little fire kindles!" (James 3:3-5).

A human tongue is a small part of our bodies. Still, it's powerful because it directs the course of our lives. Like a bit in a horse's mouth or a small rudder on a huge ship, our tongue sets our life's destination.

"And the tongue *is* a fire, a world of iniquity. The tongue is so set among our members that it defiles the whole body and sets on fire the course of nature; and it is set on fire by hell. For every kind of beast and bird, of reptile and crea-ture of the sea, is tamed and has been tamed by mankind. But no man can tame the tongue. *It is* an unruly evil, full of deadly poison"

(James 3:6-8).

Man can't tame his own tongue, but God can. That's why He told Joshua to speak and think on His words. That's why God told me to say, "I'm blessed, I'm beautiful and I'm prosperous."

TONI'S TAKE

As God taught me about His Word of Faith that begins on the inside of us, I heard ministers say things like, "If you can't see it, you'll never possess it."

One of my earliest memories of using my imagination to see what God promised is when He instructed me to say, "I'm blessed, I'm beautiful, and I'm prosperous."

In the natural I was anything but prosperous. I had such low regard for myself I didn't think there was anything beautiful about me. I wanted to experience what it meant to be blessed, but there was little evidence of what a blessed life looked like in my world.

The phrase, "I'm blessed, I'm beautiful and I'm prosperous," came as a rhema word from the Lord. It came from the Spirit of God to my spirit. It was my choice to obey what He said. As I began saying, *I'm blessed, beautiful and prosperous,* a funny thing happened. I started seeing myself *blessed, beautiful and prosperous.*

A mental shift took place. I began to see myself beyond my human limitations. I caught myself dreaming of a better future. The word from the Lord began cleaning out my old downcast mentality and lifted me out of the pit I was in. A better life didn't take shape in the natural overnight. That took a little patience.

Sadly, our tongues can also set our entire lives on fire. Holy Spirit worked with me as I spoke words that agreed with what God said about me to put out some of the fires in my life.

According to James, if we're talking sickness, failure, and defeat, we'll get sickness, failure, and defeat. If we want the results Jesus promised, we need to speak words that agree with God's Word. I learned a whole new vocabulary with this revelation. As I started talking blessed, beautiful, and prosperous, it got inside of me. I began believing and seeing blessed, beautiful, and prosperous manifesting in my life.

GOD'S PERSPECTIVE

Andrew Wommack, Bible teacher and founder of Charis Bible College, says, "Imagination is the dynamo, the power source of life."[1]

I've had the opportunity to hear Wommack teach about our imagination. In his book he quoted the King James Version of Psalm 103:14: "For he knoweth our frame; he remembereth that we are dust." Wommack explains that the word *"frame"* in this verse was translated *"imagination"* or *"imaginations"* five other times in the Old Testament.[2]

He said, "Our imagination is the frame or spine of our existence. It's the doorway to our potential and affects the way we view life (Proverbs 23:7)."[3]

When we speak and meditate the Word of God, it forms an image on the inside of us. It changes how we see ourselves and the way we view life. Seeing ourselves as God sees us is what creates lasting change. Engaging our imagination is an important part of achieving our God given potential and destiny.

TONI'S IMAGINATION AT WORK

Over time, my agreement with *blessed, beautiful, and prosperous,* created an image inside of me. God gave me a vision of what I looked like in the spirit. I was beautiful and radiant as I danced and twirled on a large boulder. To this day, I pause, and, in my imagination, I see how happy and graceful I looked as I danced on the hope my salvation promised. I was beautiful. I am still beautiful. I am loved. You are too.

The way I saw myself in the natural continued to improve. But it all began when I was obedient to do what God said to do.

I noticed that my money seemed to stretch further, too. God's Word changed what I experienced in my life. I'm not talking about positive thinking, which can slip away in a gust of opposition. There is supernatural power within God's Word to make lasting changes in our lives. His words are Spirit and they are life (John 6:63). His words make us stronger than the storms.

POWER IN THE WORD

Many of God's people talk like the devil. They're just as sick and poor as those who've never received salvation through

Jesus Christ. They remain mentally, physically, emotionally, and financially poor. I've heard ministers beg on television for money because they can't pay their bills. Financial lack is a perfect storm. Perfect as in having everything needed to destroy your life.

God promises abundance. He promises success. Just like He promised Joshua (Joshua 1:8, Deuteronomy 31:6), God also promises to never leave us or forsake us in the New Testament (Hebrews 13:5). But that doesn't change the requirement of doing things His way. We follow His instructions of hearing, obeying and putting our faith in God.

Paul said, "For I am not ashamed of the gospel of Christ, for it is the power of God to salvation for everyone who believes, for the Jew first and also for the Greek" (Romans 1:16).

The gospel is the power of God. The power of God provides eternal salvation for everyone who believes. Salvation includes saving us from whatever we need saving from while we live here on the earth before heaven. That includes storms.

Paul used the Greek word *soteria*, that translators rendered salvation. *Soteria* means, "rescue or safety (phys. or mor.): deliver, health, salvation, save, saving."[4] When we get to Heaven, we won't need deliverance, rescuing or provision for health or prosperity. There won't be any storms in heaven. These benefits are for us while we live in the earth where we face storms.

CHAPTER 9

God Works with His Word

W henever there was an issue while John and I were building a home, our contractor asked, "What does the blueprint say?"

God works with His blueprint, which is His Word, the Bible. Whenever we have a question or if an issue comes up, we should see what it says. The wise man built on his foundation by constructing what the blueprint demanded, not just any way he wanted. When we follow the blueprint, we'll be successful and thrive through the storms.

"Now to Him who is able to do exceedingly abundantly above all that we ask or think, according to the power that works in us" (Ephesians 3:20).

How does this Scripture say that God is able to do the "exceedingly abundantly" in our lives? According to the power that works in us.

Hebrews 1:3 tells us that God "…upholds all things by the word of His power…"

God supports everything in the universe by what isn't evident to our five senses. That includes you and me. If we want the "exceedingly abundantly" in our lives, we need to speak and meditate on the Word of God's power.

The Bible is the Word of His power that He's given us. That's why throughout this book I reinforce the need for you to put God's Word into your heart. God's ability to do the "exceedingly abundantly" in each of our individual lives is conditional.

This next teaching of Jesus is also conditional. Jesus said that He came "…that they may have life, and that they may have *it* more abundantly" (John 10:10). The word *may*, expresses the possibility of having. It's not a guarantee.

If we want to be strong in Him and the power of His might the Word must dwell within us and come out of our mouths in agreement with what He says.

Only those who build wise will reach the exceeding abundant life that's available to us. Only the wise builders will survive the storms.

That's why two people can grow up in the same church, hearing the same faith message, yet only the one who hears, believes and is a doer of God's Word will have abundance. The person who is a hearer only, forfeits the abundant life.

In Isaiah, God gives us an explanation of how His Word functions.

"For as the rain comes down, and the snow from heaven, And do not return there, But water the earth, And make it bring forth and bud, That it may give seed to the sower And bread to the eater" (Isaiah 55:10).

God's Word is like the rain and snow that waters the earth to produce a harvest. When God's Word lives in us, and we speak His Words in faith, God says His Words supply our needs. God's Word accomplishes their purpose as we saw with Joshua. God provides us with tremendous PPE promises for all things pertaining to life.

There's power in God's Word to yield a harvest that's full of seed for additional harvests. There's no apple seed without the apple. The Word produces the harvest plus more seed for "exceedingly abundantly" more.

Here's the next verse: "So shall My word be that goes forth from My mouth; It shall not return to Me void, but it shall accomplish that what I please, And it shall prosper in the thing for which I sent it" (Isaiah 55:11).

God promises that His Word doesn't return to Him without accomplishing what He said it would produce.

We might say, "I see in Your Word, Father, that You've promised no weapon formed against me will prosper (Isaiah 54:17). Thank You for your Word and as I send it back to You, I believe it will accomplish Your purpose in my life. I believe You are faithful. Thank You Father that Your desire is that no weapon formed against me shall prosper. That's my desire too."

No weapon formed against me shall prosper.

No weapon formed against me shall prosper.

No weapon formed against me shall prosper.

And you say it and you believe it again and again, day after day, month after month and when the need arises, you'll have the faith to trust God through the storm. That's when you'll see the evidence of God's promises in your life. You choose to believe what God says over what your circumstances scream at you. But here's the thing, you can't live like the devil and say a few words and get your circumstances straightened out. Don't let the devil deceive you. God will not be mocked (Galatians 6:7).

We submit to what the Bible says. We resist Satan's works of stealing, killing and destroying both in our lives and in our speech. The duck's prints come as lack, poverty, sickness, ignorance of what God says, and the list goes on. Stopping the devil's works in our bodies, lives, families, cities, schools, and world—that is spiritual warfare. That's one reason God gave us a battle plan in His blueprint to follow. We have God's strategy for success.

Just because diabetes, irritable bowel disease, a virus, an inability to pay your bills or whatever, starts quacking, it doesn't mean you have to take it. If you're living in sin, ask God to forgive you. Repent, straighten-up your behavior and get on the right path. Draw close to God and resist the works of the devil and he'll flee from you.

TONI'S TAKE

The wind warred with me as I tugged on the bank door. John pulled the door open, and we walked to the bank teller's window. We needed to establish an account as we prepared to move to the farm we'd purchased in rural Oklahoma. It was the mid-nineties and we'd only been married a few years.

I clicked the heels of my red boots together. Tapping my heels like Dorothy did in the *Wizard of Oz* while saying or thinking, *there's no place like home*, was my habit. I'd longed for a home but had never seemed to find one. I desired somewhere I could feel comfortable, a place where I belonged and where I fit. I believe the place we call home should be more than where we go after a long day at work. I was hopeful I'd find that warm and cozy feeling I was looking for at the farm that once belonged to John's grandparents.

Standing at the bank's counter, I sneezed.

The teller looked at me with eager attention and asked, "Are you taking it?"

John rolled his eyes. I saw his chest expand as he took a deep breath. He probably thought, *here we go again*. Can't take this woman anywhere. His body language should have been my tip-off that I was missing something. It wasn't.

I paused a moment and said, "I'm taking all the healing I can get."

The atmosphere changed as the teller drew her body backward, and away from the cubicle's opening. Bewilderment and disgust flashed across her face. She didn't comment, but her tight-lipped expression said, *Well, I never!*

I thought that made us even. I'd never heard such a question before. John informed me afterward that when I sneeze and someone asks, "Are you taking it?" they mean are you taking a cold.

"No! I'm not taking a cold! Just because the devil offers sickness doesn't mean I'm taking it. I'm not taking anything the devil offers."

John spent summers and some school years at the farm where we were moving. He'd learned how to bail and toss hay instead of working out at the gym. He was such a good athlete he could've had his photo on a cereal box. As a martial artist, he won many gold medals. He was a champion bull and bronc rider who could handle a bull for a full eight seconds. But he had trouble with a hundred-pound woman of faith.

I recall phone calls he'd received asking, "Can't you control your wife?"

Once I heard him reply, "Here," as he thrust his arm out as if he were handing me over, "You try it!"

LET FAITH TALK

John did have his hands full. After I began a relationship with the Lord, He brought me into a Word of Faith environment and taught me how to live life by faith. That's how I got my new life. Although John was a believer in Christ, he'd never heard the Word of Faith message or about the power of our words before he met me.

Faith people have a different way of talking. We intend to think God's thoughts and therefore we act—peculiar to some folks. We know that we don't have to take anything the devil dishes out. But knowing that we don't have to take the devil's garbage isn't enough. We must know how to make that a reality in our lives. We must operate in that spiritual knowledge and walk it out in wisdom. From experience, I can tell you that we get on the nerves of those who don't understand the principles that help us maintain the testimony of our faith and our thought-life.

As we draw close to God, releasing His Words from our mouth against whatever the devil offers, which is any part of the curse—spiritual death, poverty, sickness and disease—he flees. Our job is to stay close to God, and resist what the devil offers. Resisting is spiritual warfare. I had to learn this art of the warrior.

I had to learn how to fight the good fight of faith to retain the victory that Jesus died to give me if I wanted to thrive in my life. That took time. A lack of knowledge cost me some battles along the way.

Warriors don't give up and quit. The good fight of faith is one God equips us to win if we don't quit. We can't let the devil, symptoms, or a bank teller talk us out of what belongs to us in Christ. Being healthy and whole belonged to me. When symptoms or uninformed people talk sickness, disease, lack and disaster to faith people, faith people talk back.

"Therefore, submit to God. Resist the devil and he will flee from you" (James 4:7).

That's a great Scripture to build with. The Bible is full of essential building blocks that teach us how to be more powerful than the devil's attack.

Many people attempt to resist the work of the devil without first submitting to God. A wise warrior knows it won't work that way. We can't just try resisting the devil and expect the God kind of results without committing to the entire verse.

Resisting without drawing close to God will cost you battles. It will create cracks in your building. Cracks hinder confidence in your faith and opens doors to the devil.

Referring to Jesus, Paul writes, "Who hath delivered us from the power of darkness and translated us into the kingdom of his dear Son: In whom we have redemption through his blood, even the forgiveness of sins" (Colossians 1:13-14 KJV).

We've been delivered from the power of darkness by the Blood of Jesus. It's only through a relationship with Him that we can stand strong. Drawing close to Jesus provides protection against the intensity of the curse that the devil fuels against us.

Revelation 12:12 tells us that the devil knows his time on the earth is about to end. That's why he is coming down on us during these end times with such great wrath. He has every intention of sending storms our way.

We must be wiser than the devil and those who live in the world. "Those who are wise shall shine…" (Daniel 12:3). It's time. All of God's kids should rise and shine.

TONI'S TAKE

I don't recall anyone ever giving me a book when I was a kid. I didn't become a reader until after I had two daughters and purchased a Bible when I was in my late twenties. Many people say, "I'm just not a reader." Well, you have to become a student of the Bible. Reading the Bible is non-negotiable. I know of people who don't read books, but they read a lot of other things: instruction manuals, recipes, menus, information on social media and t-shirts. Ask God for help.

Don't depend on others to tell you what God says. Allow Holy Spirit to open your eyes to God's Truth. Ask Him to point out areas where you may have missed it. He'll help you understand, as well as grow to the next level. He's on your side and He wants you to succeed.

Yes, I know that takes a lot of effort. But Jesus said we have to build. Diligence pays off with a life that's stronger than the storms. Start with reading one chapter a day. Begin with John, chapter one. Read that one chapter every day for several days or a month. That one chapter brings light about Who Jesus is. Spread reading that chapter out over a few days if necessary.

The Word of God brings light so that we will know the hope of our calling (Ephesians 1:18). Our calling includes abundance and staying stronger than any storm. Remember, God carries His power out in our lives through His Word. Two to five minutes a day is all you need to get started, then build from there.

CHAPTER 10

The Word Makes Us Strong

O ver time I realized that I couldn't separate Jesus from the Word. They're one and the same but in different forms. God provided everything we could ever need or desire, and it all comes through Jesus, the Word. Nothing is made without Him (John 1:3).

When we read the Bible, we're spending time with Jesus. The first time I read John chapter one with understanding I was speechless. I knew what I heard the Word say, but it was so beyond my comprehension.

"In the beginning was the Word, and the Word was with God, and the Word was God" (John 1:1 KJV). After a long pause I continued reading through the chapter. Verse fourteen stopped me in my tracks. "And the Word was made flesh and dwelt among us, (and we beheld his glory, the glory as the only begotten of the Father,) full of grace and truth" (John 1:14 KJV).

Jesus is the Word!

I didn't have words or thoughts to help me process this information. I was so caught up in the revelation of the moment that it was as if time stood still. This was one of my first experiences of the Word lighting me up.

Months later, a new acquaintance introduced me to the pastor of her church. I was a little nervous. I didn't have a pastor as the Lord hadn't led me to a church yet. Her pastor gave me an opportunity to ask him a question. I jumped at the chance.

Referring to the first chapter of John, I asked, "Is this saying that Jesus is God?"

His answer of course was yes. It felt exhilarating to get something right. I saw something in the Word! And although I couldn't explain how I understood it, I got it.

Has that ever happened to you?

God gave me revelation knowledge. It was much like a stadium light beaming on my path or a giant piece of a puzzle clicking into place. Peter received revelation light when he knew Jesus was the Christ.

"The entrance of Your words gives light; It gives understanding to the simple" (Psalm 119:130).

No question about it. I was simple.

Something similar happened when I read Genesis 1:26. I became so excited when I realized God wasn't alone.

"And God said, Let us make man in our image, after our likeness…" (KJV).

I shouted, "God! Who was with You? Who were you talking to? Us? Who is Us? Let Us make man?"

I've been in love with the Word of God from the time I first began reading the Bible. I've been lost to everything except the Word since 1984. Before long, I was reading my Bible for hours. I still do.

As God said in Genesis 1:3, Light, be! Which, by the way, was another Scripture that lit me up. God called for Light before the sun, moon and stars made their appearance.

That's how it works. All you have to do is start reading the Word with Holy Spirit. He'll unveil an amazing God that you never expected or imagined. He'll lead you to adventures of a lifetime.

THE WORD BECAME FLESH

The Word is very interesting. The Bible tells us that the Word became Jesus, born of the Virgin Mary, that dwelt among us (John 1:14).

He, Jesus the Word, made all things. The Word made the trees, the sun, the moon, the sky, the animal and sea life, and all things that exist. The Word made you and me. You can read the story in the first two chapters of Genesis. Chapter three is about how man fell into enemy hands.

When His kids were kidnapped and hijacked by Satan, the evil warlord, God sent His Word and solved the problem. Nothing happens without the Word. When you're facing a storm it's the Word, Jesus, Who will rescue you.

THE BASICS

Without the Word, nothing is made or will ever be made. The Word became flesh and dwelt among us as Jesus. Either directly or indirectly, the Word became everything we see in the world.

Let's use the example of our computer screen. Every material used to create it came into existence by the Word. The Word became the Bible that we hold in our hands. It's the Word that will become whatever you need. It's the Word that will make you stronger than sickness, disease, lack, pandemics and storms. In fact, meditating Psalm 91:10 can build our faith to the extent that a plague won't faze or harm us. That doesn't negate our bodies needs for nutrients. Nor are we eliminating common sense.

Even the vitamins and minerals we need began in the beginning with the Word (Genesis Chapter One). Jesus said it's the wise man who builds by hearing and doing what He— the Word says. Nothing happens without the Word. Remember though, believing and trusting in God's faithfulness is implied and should be understood.

The basic 101 application for living by faith is to find God's PPE promise from the Bible that supplies what you need and start building. God works with His Word.

Without the Word, nothing was created (John 1:3). Not one change happened, not one thing came into being in this world that didn't come through the Word.

Think about it. Because God so loved the world, He sent His Word (John 3:16 my paraphrase).

God's angel delivered a *Word* from God to Mary. Mary knew from the *Word* (Scriptures) that a virgin would conceive (Isaiah 7:14). Throughout the Bible the *Word* about Jesus had been spoken and recorded. When Mary agreed with the *Word*, the *Word* through the power of Holy Spirit impregnated her. That *Word* grew into the Incarnate Body of Jesus. When Mary gave birth, Jesus the *Word* became flesh (John 1:14). Speaking words is how God created everything. We can choose to do the same.

God needed a Savior to rescue man from the devil's clutches, so He sent His Word. That's how God meets our need. He spoke His Word and recorded it in His blueprint, the Bible. Our job is to get into agreement with what God said and hold tight. The Word becomes our answer to everything including rescuing us from the storms.

Jesus is the One who said that man wouldn't live by bread alone but by every Word that proceeds from the mouth of God (Matthew 4:4). If we want the ability to rise above the storms of life, and above the level where the world lives, we must start with God's Word.

Whatever you need—healing, a new liver, or lungs because you smoked for twenty years, deliverance and protection, or whatever—it comes through the Word that promises healing, a new organ, restoration, deliverance and protection. The Holy Spirit hovers over God's Word to perform it just like He did in Genesis 1:2. Just like He did with Mary (Luke 1:35). Just like He did throughout Jesus's ministry on earth.

TONI'S TAKE

I want to take the Word being the answer to everything, down to the ridiculous.

God has turned His Word into a stringer of hand carved, wooden fish that I hang on my fireplace tools. The manifestation of the fish began with the Word of faith when I prayed. I liked the stringer of fish when I saw them at the store. I just wasn't willing to pay $50 plus tax. In the 1990's that was a lot of money for fish. So, based on Mark 11:22-24, I asked God for them. I began thanking Him for them. Soon, the store had a clearance sale.

Guess what? The fish were on the closeout table, and I paid one dollar for them.

The Word *becomes* the answer to our needs and desires. Mary, the mother of Jesus, knew that. Before Jesus turned water into wine at the wedding at Cana, she told the servants, "…Whatever He says to you, do it" (John 2:5).

The Word becomes whatever we need.

CHAPTER 11

Four Witnesses

The foundation is the most important part of building a house. Get it wrong and the house can have expensive and endless problems. It can even collapse. Without a rock-solid foundation, at some point our lives will crumble. Either here on the earth or when we enter our forever destination. Jesus is the Word. That means that the Word of God is the foundation for everything that pertains to life.

Our foundation must be trustworthy. God is as trustworthy as it gets. It's wisdom to build our lives God's way so we're building spiritually strong on that foundation and upward. We trust that God sent Jesus to rescue us. Even though we can't see heaven, we believe we're going there one day.

Do we trust His faithfulness for taking care of us while we're here on earth amidst the things that we can see? Or are we just hopeful that He will, while at the same time, we're hedging our bets, relying more on our physical senses, talents, and intellect than on Him? We can have absolute trust in our God, our Rock-solid foundation.

As we look at God's faithfulness, we'll take the help of four witnesses. These details are so important to our longevity that I want to make sure you're hearing what Jesus is saying. When the Lord showed me this, I understood why not all His kids survived when storms hit. It's one of those building details that can't be overlooked. Consider this next section as strict code enforcement when building. But first, let's revisit our foundation scripture.

"**Therefore, whosoever hears these sayings of Mine, and does them**, I will liken him unto a wise man who built his house on the rock: and the rain descended, the floods came, and the winds blew and beat on that house; and it did not fall, for it was founded on the rock" (Matthew 7:24-25 emphasis mine).

Jesus said that when the winds huffed and puffed and blew, the wise man survived because he anchored his life into the Rock and built. The pastor didn't build for him. The televangelist didn't do the building. The wise man's house wasn't built by family tradition and passed down from generation to generation. It wasn't built on religious doctrine, catechism, or hearsay.

The wise man built on the Rock with his own materials of hearing, believing, and doing what Jesus said. The pastor, priests, the man's parents, and the televangelist may have provided some building materials, but they didn't do the building for him. Likewise, all I can do is provide information and share the knowledge and wisdom I've gained over the years. The Master Builder will help you get supernatural results as you build according to His blueprint.

WITNESS ONE: THE YOUNG PETER

Who is Jesus to you?

Peter discovered the importance of knowing the identity of Jesus. When Jesus asked the disciples who they thought He was, Peter proclaimed Jesus as "…the Christ, the Son of the living God." (Matthew 16:15-16).

Jesus commended Peter for having the right answer, which flesh, and blood hadn't provided (verse 17). The right answer came through revelation knowledge revealed to him by Father God. Peter didn't get his information from his own reasoning or five physical senses. He didn't receive his information from a religious institution. He received insight from God that gave him the ability to operate on a higher level than his peers. Revelation from God takes us to a higher spiritual operating level that He made available.

Jesus said, "And I say also unto thee, that thou art Peter, and upon this rock I will build my church; and the gates of hell shall not prevail against it" (Matthew 16:18 KJV).

As one of the men who penned the New Testament, Peter is one of many who helps us build on that rock. When Jesus said that He'd build His church on the rock, He was referring to Christ Himself. Jesus said He would build His church on this immovable, indisputable rock of revelation knowledge that came directly from the Spirit of God that Jesus is the Christ.

An unmistakable eyewitness that we can't deny is that in both Old and New Testaments, God and Jesus are often referred to as the Rock. Rock, as in the strong and unmovable boulder kind. The kind of rock-solid foundation we need to anchor into in order to build strong faith and confidence. We have to trust God's faithfulness as we'd trust the immovability of a giant boulder.

"For no other foundation can anyone lay than that which is laid, which is Jesus Christ" (1 Corinthians 3:11).

Revelation knowledge is revealed by the Spirit of God directly to our spiritual heart. It's not knowledge gained through the senses or intellect. God's Truth lights us up and comes alive on the inside of us.

Receiving revelation knowledge from God is how Jesus expects us to live. Spending time in God's Word brings light to our understanding that enables us to build unshakable confidence in God's faithfulness. That's when the storms, or the gates of hell shall not prevail against us. God's Truth becomes so strong within, the devil can't beat it out of us and the evidence of being more than conquerors through Christ becomes evident for all to see.

"Yet in all these things we are more than conquerors through Him who loved us" (Romans 8:37).

Paul was referring to the storms of tribulation, distress, persecution, famine, nakedness, peril and swords (36), when he said we are more than conquerors. Paul was fully persuaded that no storm and no devil would prevail against him.

"For I am persuaded that neither death nor life, nor angels nor principalities nor powers, nor things present nor things to come, nor height nor depth, nor any other created thing, shall be able to separate us from the love of God which is in Christ Jesus our Lord" (Romans 8:38-39).

Who do you say Jesus is? Who do you know Him as? Is Jesus Christ your Rock?

WITNESS TWO: THE APOSTLE PAUL

There's only one Rock with that kind of immoveable integrity, and the Apostle Paul testifies to Him. The same Rock that Jesus told Peter He would build His church upon.

"As it is written, Behold I am laying in Zion **a Stone that will make men stumble, a Rock that will make them fall**; but he who believes in Him [who adheres to, trusts in, and relies on Him] shall not be put to shame nor be disappointed in his expectations" (Romans 9:33 AMPC emphasis mine).

We know that God sent Him—Jesus, the Word, the Rock of our foundation because He loved the world, and so that all who would believe on Him would be saved (John 3:16).

In His written Word, God has made it clear that His desire is for all men to be saved and come to the knowledge of the Truth (1 Timothy 2:4).

Therefore, we know that God did not send Jesus to make anyone fall, stumble, or fail to receive Him as Savior. Not just for after our bodies die, but to also trust and lean on Him for the salvation He alone provides while we live here in the world. Now, does this Rock make men fall and stumble? Yes, He does. But that's not God's will. God's will is that all people believe in Him, and in all that He died to give.

Let's look at the second half of that verse: "...but he who believes in Him [who adheres to, trusts in, and relies on Him] shall not be put to shame nor be disappointed in his expectations."

Salvation is for those who believe. Whether it's for going to heaven or before. People stumble and fall when they either refuse to believe in Him or lack understanding of what to believe. The depth of what God has provided through salvation is staggering. There are many essential building tools that we need knowledge and understanding about to build strong.

WITNESS THREE: THE MATURE PETER

"And, A Stone that will cause stumbling and a Rock that will give [men] offense; they stumble because they disobey and disbelieve [God's] Word, as those [who reject Him] were destined (appointed) to do" (1 Peter 2: 8 AMPC).

Anyone who refuses to believe in Jesus will trip because that's what unbelievers are destined to do. Unbelievers have no Light to walk in. They have no power for change. They have no spiritual weapons against the bringer of storms. They live at the whim of the devil and are taken captive by him at his will.

This is where I want you to pay particular attention. Peter says that for God's kids, disobeying and disbelieving God's Word produces the same results as an unbeliever gets.

The Bible was written to God's kids. In the first epistle of Peter, he was writing to those who were sanctified by the Spirit (verse 1). Peter isn't speaking to those who've rejected Jesus as Savior and haven't received salvation. He's telling the believers in the Lord that unless they believe what God says, they'll get the same results as those who don't even believe in Jesus.

From our foundation scripture we know that Jesus said the wise man will hear and obey God's Word. Jesus taught that the man who isn't offended because of Him shall be blessed (Matthew 11:6).

According to Kenneth and Gloria Copeland, the word *blessed* is an empowerment to prosper. "The blessing of the Lord makes one rich, And He adds no sorrow with it" (Proverbs 10:22).

Doesn't that sound like being stronger than the storm of poverty? Being rich in God's wisdom will make you stronger than the storms of sickness and disease.

Blessed is the positive side of tenacity where the Word of God is concerned. There's a negative side as well. Many Christians use bulldog resistance against changing their wrong beliefs and wrong doctrines. They're tenacious in their desire to hold onto the doctrines of men instead of believing what God says. Many are steadfast in their refusal to let go of their dogma that contradicts God's Truth. Some of them are in the pulpit. Some are on television across the globe. That's why we must know for ourselves what the Bible says. Allowing anyone other than the Word Himself to dictate what we believe doesn't make a wise builder.

First Peter 2:8 also proves that no one is destined or appointed to reject Jesus. It's a choice each of us make. We choose our own eternal destiny.

Jesus died for everyone, not just those who would choose to believe in Him. One of the lies Satan has filled the minds of people with is that it's not God's will for all to be saved. Not just saved for Heaven but saved from the storms associated with life while we live in this world.

Believers or non-believers alike are destined and appointed to stumble and fall when they disobey or disbelieve God's Word. Disbelieving God comes at a high cost. Many don't survive the storms.

God still loves all who refuse to believe Him. Those who are His kids will still go to Heaven when they die. But while on the earth they'll fare the same as an unbeliever who never received Jesus as Savior. Selah that for a moment.

In my opinion that's one reason we don't see much difference between the church and the world today. Family discord, pre-mature death, sickness, disease, lack and calamity is widespread in the church and among those who don't even believe in Jesus as their Savior.

If you want to be stronger than the storms, read the Word for yourself and choose to believe God and obey.

WITNESS FOUR: THE ROCK AND MOSES

The Israelites needed water in Numbers, Chapter 20. God told Moses to take his rod, the same rod that God had wrought many miracles, and gather with Aaron and the congregation of people. God told Moses that in front of the people, he was to speak to the rock to give water. Instead, Moses struck the rock with his rod—twice.

"Then the Lord spoke to Moses and Aaron, "Because you did not believe Me, to hallow Me in the eyes of the children of Israel, therefore you shall not bring this assembly into the land which I have given them" (Numbers 20:12).

God said they didn't believe Him. God said use your words and speak to the rock. Instead, Moses acted in his own strength. It's possible that Moses had grown comfortable and trusted in his rod and how he thought God did things. Maybe he had his faith in the rod instead of in God. Moses may have been tired and frustrated. He may have been relying on his own logic and reasoning. *Who gets water from a rock?*

Regardless of why Moses struck the rock, God saw his disobedience as unbelief.

The Israelite's storm was a lack of water. God wanted the people to see that all Moses had to do was speak to the rock and He would provide supernatural results. Moses wanted to do things the way he'd always done them, in his own strength and might.

Moses disobeyed and failed to take what God said to heart, which is what we just read in 1 Peter 2:8. Those who disobey and disbelieve God's Word, fare the same as those who reject Him. The price Moses paid for failing to take God at His Word was the Promised Land. The price we pay today for not believing God are His PPE promises that He's made to us.

God was trying to establish a principle in the eyes of the Israelites. Moses robbed God of the opportunity to show His faithfulness to the people. His unbelief and disobedience cost those whom he was responsible for the ability to see God's power.

TONI'S TAKE

We've talked about the power in our tongues to change our destiny. I've shared two of my stories about speaking to tornados. I speak to a lot of things including sickness, disease, money, my body, demons—because God told us to say what we want. The salvation we receive through Jesus began with the Word of God when we believed in our heart and said words. That's still God's basic building principle and will never change.

The next verses should be familiar. The emphasis on the words 'say' are mine. This is what Jesus said. It's our choice to believe what He says or not.

"Have faith in God. For assuredly, I say to you, whoever **says** to this mountain, 'Be removed and be cast into the sea,' and does not doubt in his heart, but believes that those things he **says** will be done, he will have whatever he **says**. Therefore, I say to you, whatever things you ask when you pray, believe that you receive *them*, and you will have *them*" (Mark 11:22-24).

Moses needed water from the rock to quench the people's thirst. Thank God He is merciful and full of love. God still allowed water to come from the rock. But Moses forfeited the Promised Land. We too can lose access to God's promises when we fail to follow instructions. We have to train ourselves in God's ways.

TONI'S BLUNT TAKE

Christians who are surrounded by storms and then run to God are going to be in trouble if they haven't been wise builders. Because many lack understanding some will blame God for the storm or decide for themselves that it wasn't God's will for them to survive. That contradicts the scriptures I've brought out in this book. Without faith in God and following His way of doing things we limit His ability like the children of Israel limited Him.

"How often they provoked Him in the wilderness and grieved Him in the desert! Yes, again and again they tempted God, and limited the Holy One of Israel" (Psalm 78:40-41).

Unbelief limits God. He will still do as much as He can to help us. However, He's limited when we fail to believe what He says. When storms hit, having failed to build wise is one reason bad things happen to God's kids. They'll still go to Heaven if they die in the storm—and many do die premature deaths because they haven't built wise on their foundations.

Being stronger than the storms doesn't mean that as believers we'll do everything perfectly, or that we'll never miss it or never fail. At times we all limit God—me included.

We must remember guilt or condemnation is not from God. God loves us and regardless of what happens in life, God never changes. We trust His promises and faithfulness as we continue following the teachings of Jesus. We hear what He says and do it trusting God will do what He says He will do. Melanie and Vicki heard from God, trusted and prayed in the spirit. Praying in the spirit takes limits off of God and is always powerful.

I know that when we're trusting God, doing all that we know to do, He picks up our slack. He meets us where we are, upholds us and helps us be the overcomers and more than conquerors that He's called us to be. God is always for us.

"The LORD is on my side; I will not fear…" (Psalm 118:6).

Therefore, faring the same as an unbeliever shouldn't be the norm. It shouldn't be our accepted standard. Jesus died a horrific death to redeem us from the hand of the devil. Jesus died and rose from the grave to show us God's faithfulness. It's time that God's kids take back what the devil has stolen. It's time that God's kids fare better than those who don't even belong to Him.

What do you say?

PETER, PAUL, AND ME

Both Peter and Paul were men who functioned above the standard that average men could operate.

That level is available to us today. That's how I got my new life.

Peter literally spent time with the Word Incarnate, meaning Jesus the Word who became flesh. Paul spent time in the presence of Jesus (1 Corinthians 9:1) and received revelation straight from the Master (Galatians 1:11-12, Ephesians 3:3) to write most of the New Testament. I spent time with Jesus through the Bible, the Word of God in written form.

The only thing I was ever good at doing was what I was told to do. Becoming a doer of the Word is where that kind of obedience paid off. It helped me build a life that the gates of hell—storms, disasters, sickness, pandemics, lack, and poverty—could not prevail against.

We're nearing the finish line. Man's lease on the earth is about to expire. The battles we face are between Light and darkness. It's going to take obedience to the Word of God to build strong. It's going to take tenacity to win. The kind of tenacity Jesus had. The kind of determination Peter and Paul had. This is a fight to the finish. Satan won't back off unless we make him.

Paul compares life to being in a race and he tells us to run our race to win (1 Corinthians 9:24). We have to be all in. Like in the movie "Ford VS Ferrari." Ken Miles was all in— until he got to the finish line.

In the movie, Henry Ford II, set out to prove that he was as good as his grandfather, the founder of Ford Motor Company. Engines roared, rpms kicked in and personal demons came out of hiding when Junior decided he could build a Ford race car that would beat Enzo Ferrari at the 24 Hours of Le Mans in France in 1966.

Ford teamed a bunch of hot shot race car drivers and mechanics with his wealthy, prideful and sneaky corporate executives. Miles had no fear of speed, or the suits bent on taking him down.

Miles left a lot of skid marks as he fought and stood up against the chain of command that wanted to keep him off the track. He maintained his position as the Ford driver. But Miles was a nice guy, and in the end, he forfeited his victory and let the win be stolen from him. I'm not saying there's anything wrong with being a team player. But when you're in a race, you're in it to win.

CHRISTIAN RACE

Unlike the Le Mans, where drivers vie for the win, Christians don't compete with each other. We're supposed to shore each other up. As Christ followers we set aside the weights—anything that knocks us off course and opposes who we are in Christ. We run our race on the courses of our individual lives. Weights could be a lack of personal, God centered boundaries. It could be distractions, bad habits or even disobedience and unbelief. Sin will always zap our energy and trip us up. To win our race we need to avoid the big wrecks, and not disqualify ourselves. We want to cross the finish line well. We want Jesus to consider us wise builders in this life before we hear well done in Heaven.

Paul didn't have race cars in his day—but I bet he would have liked one. Paul said we're to train with the same focus and determination of an athlete going for the gold. "Do you not know that in a race all the runners compete, but [only] one receives the prize? So run [your race] that you may lay hold [of the prize] *and* make it yours" (1 Corinthians 9:24 AMPC).

It's going to take consistency, faith in God and determination. It's going to take the power of God to run our race, stay the course and win over the storms of life. There is no second place. Training translates spending time with the Word of God, hearing and doing what He says in faith. The choice is ours.

Satan knows his days are short on the earth. He's aggressive in his attacks against the world and Christ followers. We have to refuse to lose. We have to set aside the things that take us down and make us feel less than who the Word of God says we are. We have to be steadfast and disciplined. We can't fail to receive what the Word says belongs to us.

CHAPTER 12

The Foolish Builder

We've discussed the wise builder. Jesus had a lot
to say about the foolish builder as well.
Everyone is building something. The question
is whether we'll be wise, or foolish builders.

"But everyone who hears these sayings of Mine, and does
not do them, will be like a foolish man who built his house
on the sand: and the rain descended, the floods came, and
the winds blew and beat on that house; and it fell. And great
was its fall" (Matthew 7:26-27).

NOT AUTOMATIC

Jesus told Martha, that her sister Mary had found the one
thing that was needed—hearing His voice (Luke 10:42).
Mary spent time with the Living Word. She gave Him her
undivided attention. Martha was busy with domestic duties.
She tried, but she couldn't pull Mary away from Jesus to
help with her food preparation. Mary may have even

thought, *Good grief, Martha. Quit being so foolish. Give Jesus a couple fish and some bread and join me. Let Jesus prepare the meal.*

TONI'S TAKE

Before I began reading the Bible and attending church, I didn't know I could be stronger than life's storms. I'd never heard that Jesus did miracles or that God had promised us anything. I struggled to feed my daughters and pay rent. I may have been born again, but my life was a wreck. I was broke and broken. I didn't have any peace.

I believed in God, Jesus and Holy Spirit. However, because I lacked knowledge of what God said and didn't have a relationship with His Word, I was easy prey for the enemy.

The devil had a picnic destroying my life. I lived with an open door to him. Even by the world's standard, I didn't have the skillset to build a quality storm-proofed life that the economy or an illness wouldn't be able to devour. I lacked education and the tools necessary to build wise. My old life is a witness to the fact that God's PPE promises are not automatic. If all the promises God made us were automatic, then I wouldn't have ended up in the pit.

If God's promises were automatic, we'd never see a sick, depressed, addicted, or poor Christian. We'd never see a Christian who couldn't pay her bills, even in the middle of mass layoffs or a pandemic. We'd never see a Christian succumb to cancer or a virus if God's promises were automatic.

BUILDING WISE

We can choose to build our homes, or our lives, with a lot of different materials. The only way we can be sure what we're building will be stronger than the storms is to build with the teachings of Jesus. His teachings are His doctrine (Mark 4:2 KJV). The principles He lived by.

I started building by taking a few baby steps as I learned what the Bible said. I was determined to be a wise builder.

Never again would I be prey that the enemy could devour. As long as we have an enemy, we have to keep our guard up. As long as we live on the earth, we'll have plenty of sunny days—and some stormy ones.

You too can make the decision to be stronger than the storms.

Build wise my friend! Until we meet again,

Toni

Obtaining Your Building Permit

Before we can build anything on the Rock, we need to receive the Rock, Jesus, as our Lord and Savior. Look at the first four words of this next scripture and let them speak to your heart. They apply to everything we've talked about in this book.

"**Whoever comes to Me**, and hears My sayings and does them, I will show you whom he is like: He is like a man building a house, who dug deep and laid the foundation on the rock. And when the flood arose, the stream beat vehemently against that house, and could not shake it, for it was founded on the rock" (Luke 6:47-48 emphasis mine).

Jesus said, "Whoever comes to Me." Let His saying sink in deep. Whether you're coming to Jesus for the first time, or running to the Word during a storm, the key is coming to Jesus the Word.

The first step to hearing and doing is coming to Jesus. If you've never received Jesus as the Lord of your life, or if you're not sure that you're what the Bible calls born-again—come to Jesus now. Maybe you'd like to come to Him and recommit your life to doing things His way. You just need to say a simple prayer. The Apostles preached the Word of Faith. We have Paul's testimony of that to the Romans.

"But what does it say? "The word is near you, in your mouth and in your heart" (that is, the word of faith which we preach): **that if you confess with your mouth the Lord Jesus and believe in your heart that God has raised Him from the dead, you will be saved**" (Romans 10:8-9 emphasis mine).

Notice in the last sentence that Paul said it's with the heart that one believes. If you can't speak, then write your declaration of belief on a piece of paper and believe it from your heart.

Write or call out to God. Say out loud, "God, I believe in my heart and I confess with my mouth that Jesus is the Son of God who came in the flesh. I believe that He died in my place and that You God, raised Him from the dead. I believe that by His stripes I am healed now. I believe I am now your child. I am saved and born again by your Holy Spirit. I believe you are a forgiver and forgetter of sins. I ask you to forgive me of all my sins that are known and unknown to me. Take my life and teach me how to hear and do your sayings."

God doesn't lie. If you believe in your heart and confess Jesus as your Lord with your mouth you are now His child. He says He blots out sin and chooses not to remember (Hebrews 8:12). He does this so that He can be close to you. Now trust Him.

Holy Spirit Guidance System

Often in life it seems we lack understanding or don't know how to pray. One of the gifts God gave us for that very purpose is Holy Spirit.

Holy Spirit comes to dwell in us when we're born again. There's also an additional experience that we're privileged to enjoy. It's called the baptism of the Holy Spirit. This is when we allow ourselves to be completely immersed in Him. The difference is that at salvation, He indwells us, and at the Baptism, we immerse ourselves in Him. When we give ourselves to Holy Spirit, He gives us a special prayer language called tongues. It's the language of the spirit and the devil can't understand it.

The only requirement for receiving Holy Spirit's baptism is that we're born again. If you'd like this special gift and prayer language, pray the prayer that follows.

Say out loud: *I am now reborn and Your child Father God. I ask You for the gift of the Holy Spirit. Holy Spirit immerse me with Yourself and rise up within me as I praise God. Thank You Father for the Holy Spirit. I expect to speak in other tongues as You give me the utterance.*

Now, lift your hands toward heaven as if you were a child and you wanted your Father to pick you up. Say thank You and start praising God for Holy Spirit. Praising God might sound something like this: *Father I thank you for Jesus. Thank you for sending Holy Spirit and giving me my prayer language. You are a wonderful Father. Thank you for loving me. You are so good to me. Halleluiah, halleluiah, halleluiah...*

Keep saying *halleluiah* with your own voice. As you sense an urge coming from your belly area to your vocal cords, allow yourself to give sound to whatever you sense. As you yield your tongue, you'll speak syllables and words that are not your natural language. They'll rise up and want release from your mouth. You have to use your own voice. You have to release the utterances the same as you'd release words in a conversation. Holy Spirit won't force you. It's a gentle nudge or prompting which you allow to rise and come out of your mouth.

Don't be concerned with how it sounds. Like with our babies, God's babies don't come with a full vocabulary. I only had three little syllables at first. The sounds you make are the language Holy Spirit gives you and it will develop as you practice—every day.

You are a born again, Spirit-filled believer. Your life will never be the same. Enjoy God's armor.

If you don't have a church, I encourage you to get in a good Bible believing church where you can learn and grow. Make sure they believe the full gospel and promote the power of Jesus Christ. Don't let anyone talk you out of what Father God wants to do in your life.

Acknowledgments

I am so thankful and appreciative to those who've impacted my life through solid Biblical teaching. The Truth and principles they shared provided building materials that have helped me build a life that's stronger than the storms. Truths that have made a difference between life and death outcomes. Much of who I am today is the result of the dedication and commitment of these ministers who've taught God's uncompromised Truth from His Word.

I am also thankful for God's Wordsmiths. They've mentored and offered insights that has helped me grow as a writer and express what I believe God has called me to share in this book. To my critique group partners and editors, please accept my deepest gratitude. To my writing mentor and coach, I couldn't have don't it without you. Thank you all for the encouragement and support you've offered that has helped me accomplish what God has purposed for me.

My prayer is that the Truths in this book will provide you, dear Reader, with materials that will help you build a life that's *Stronger than the Storms.*

To God be the glory.

Notes

5. THE BRINGER OF STORMS

1. Chapter 5: The Bringer of Storms
   Spiros Zodhiates, Th.D. *The Complete Word Study New Testament, Word Study Series,* (Chattanooga, TN: AMG Publishers), "Ask, Desire," (154 and 4441).

7. DWELLING AND ABIDING

1. Chapter 7: Dwelling and Abiding
   thinklearnsucceedbook.com Dr. Caroline Leaf Section
2. Dr. Caroline Leaf, *Switch On Your Brain, The Key to Peak Happiness, Thinking, and Health,* (Grand Rapids, MI: Baker Books 2013), 34-35.
3. Dr. Caroline Leaf, *Think Learn Succeed, Understanding and Using Your Mind to Thrive at School, the Workplace, and Life* (Grand Rapids, MI: Baker Books 2018), 42.
4. Dr. Caroline Leaf, *Switch On Your Brain, The Key to Peak Happiness, Thinking, and Health,* (Grand Rapids, MI: Baker Books 2013), 34.
5. Ibid. 35.
6. Ibid. 35.
7. "Stress," (Entry 1 of 2) c, www.merriam-webster.com
8. Dr. Caroline Leaf, *Switch On Your Brain, The Key to Peak Happiness, Thinking, and Health,* (Grand Rapids, MI: Baler Books 2013), 36.

8. THE TRAINING GROUND OF HEARING AND OBEYING

1. Chapter 8: The Training Ground of Hearing and Obeying
   Andrew Wommack, *The Power of Imagination, Unlocking Your Ability to Receive From God,* (Shippensburg, PA: Harrison House Publishers, 2019) 7.
2. Ibid. 7.
3. Ibid. 7.
4. Chapter 9: God Works With His Word

Spiros Zodhiates, Th.D. *The Complete Word Study New Testament, Word Study Series,* (Chattanooga, TN: AMG Publishers, 1991), *Soteria,* (4991).

About the Author

Ask **Toni Chism** what she does, she'll smile and answer, "I work for God."

Beginning her marketplace ministry, Toni purchased Bibles at garage sales and gave them to those she shared Jesus with. Today, she leads women into a position of spiritual strength so they can receive everything Jesus died to give.

Word of Faith Warrior, certified Advanced Christian Life Coach, international speaker, teacher and author, Toni has a bachelor's degree in journalism. She's authored articles, short stories and resources that have appeared in newspapers, magazines and books. She's the winner of the prestigious 2019 WriterCon Inspirational Writing Contest.

The wife of John, Toni lives in Oklahoma, drinks domestic coffee and writes from her log cabin in the woods that John planted for her. She has two daughters and eight grandchildren who call her Honey.

You can register for news, book release dates and more by opting-in on her email registry. Toni doesn't like her inbox bombarded and she'll never overload yours.

Visit Toni at www.tonichism.com.

SPIRITUAL WARFARE IS NOT A DRILL.

It's time to armor-up.

Download your FREE Spiritual Warrior Strategy at ToniChism.com.

www.ingramcontent.com/pod-product-compliance
Lightning Source LLC
Chambersburg PA
CBHW060534130626
46553CB00002B/745